WE FALL DOWN BUT WE GET UP
THE PRODIGAL SON

**A True Story Written by
Pastor Grayling E. Ferrand**

About the Author

Grayling E. Ferrand is a born-again Christian and, the Pastor/founder of Reaching Across the World Ministries, Inc. whose vision is: "Uplifting Humanity, One Soul at a Time," and whose mission is "To Provide Faith-based Human Services Programs Geared Toward Eradicating Social Ills Affecting Humanity." Pastor Ferrand initially served as an amore bearer, and later deacon at the Temple of Blessings Church of God in Christ under the leadership of Pastor David W. Grayson, Jr. Under the Holy Spirit, he was led to incorporate RAW Ministries. He felt that he'd been called since the creation of time. His mother-in-law, Pastor Frieda Harrison of Jehovah Jireh Ministries, assisted him in obtaining the necessary license on the natural level.

Pastor Ferrand is presently pursuing a PhD in the field of Human Services with a Specialization in Managing Not-for-profit Agencies. As a child he was water baptized, accepted Jesus Christ as his Personal Lord and Savior, and sang in the choir; it was at the Temple of Blessings Church of God in Christ that he received the anointing of the Holy Spirit and the call to ministry in December 1999. Shortly thereafter, he married Talisa Simone Harrison. While living with her, God continued completing the work that He had started in Pastor Ferrand (Phil. 1:6). Lady Ferrand, raised in the Apostolic Faith, is his marital and spiritual partner. She provides him with the encouragement and inspiration he has always yearned for in a significant other. With her he is able to put 10,000 demons to flight.

Some of the language was left in its original form as it flowed naturally. Most times, the author did not spell out the entire word out of respect for many religious people who may read this book. It gives credence to the Pastor's understanding that one cannot be so heavenly high that he is no earthly good.

Pastor Ferrand does not want anyone of today or tomorrow to categorize other black men as being just like him with all his faults and successes. These things written are from the pastor's individual experience; it is an autobiography and testimony, and therefore should not be attributed to all black men of today.

Those wishing to further support RAW Ministries can do so by contacting us at:

Reaching Across the World Ministries, Inc.
PO Box 60254
Brooklyn, New York 11206

OR

1237 DeKalb Avenue
Brooklyn, NY 11221

E-Mail: Pastor_Ferrand@rawministries.org
Website: www.rawministries.org

All financial donations are tax deductible. Other support (i.e., technical assistance, equipment, food, clothing, employment, vehicles, etc.) is crucially needed and will be appreciated.

Clergy and others, who wish Pastor Ferrand to provide an inspirational message, please feel free to contact him. All out-of-state speaking engagements require a 30-day advance notice. Pastor Ferrand specializes in speaking in prisons, in homeless shelters, at substance abuse programs, and in college classes that focus on social and human services.

Professors who use this book for their coursework will be assisting the ministry in that 50% of the proceeds from the sale of the book will go toward RAW Ministries.

Acknowledgments

This book would not have been possible without: First and foremost, my Lord and Savior Jesus Christ, who is the head of my life. It is only through his Divine Will that my life is even sustained.

I would like to thank my wife for her patience, support and understanding and for allowing me the space and time to complete this work.

I would like to thank my mother Gloria Ferrand, and my brother Neville Barbour whose mentioning of writing his book gave me great inspiration to write my own book.

In addition to my family, I would like to thank Lola Stephens of L.Stephens Graphic Design Studio for donating the book cover. I also want to thank Aubry Padmore, my constant motivator, for his consistent and persistent support in working with the publishing team and the graphic design studio; without this phenomenal team we could not have accomplished this project. For more on this team visit www.minds-in-motion.org.

I would like to thank all who have supported me in my efforts to rebuild my life and the lives of others, one person at a time.

I thank you all so much from the bottom of my heart.

Dedications

I dedicate this book to the collective people who are the champions of the Human Struggle: to those who have died during the Diaspora and slavery, in the wars in America, and in the Attica prison riots; to those who live for the struggle now and to those who have yet to come into the existence of our struggle; to all of those children who are like the prodigal sons and daughters of today; to the parents who feel the pain of watching their loved ones suffer trials and tribulations. This book is dedicated to them all. Keep the faith and know that God is able, and His bloodstained banner still reigns.

This book is dedicated to the youth of today and tomorrow. It is hoped that when the youth of tomorrow want to know about the men of today, they will be able to find this book among the archives and annals of many others that tell the true story of the struggle and plight of today. However, I do not dedicate it more to the future generations than I do to the past or present ones but, God willing, I want whoever reads this book long after I am gone to know that they were in my prayers as often and as sincerely as those of today are. I pray now that God protects, guides, keeps, and sees them and their families through it all.

This book is dedicated to the souls of its readers: it is hoped that this book touches, inspires and guides them to do right, or deter them from doing wrong. This book will have then served its main purpose.

This book is a story of an African-American male, a prodigal son, who fell down but got up with the help of God.

I love you all. In Jesus Name,
Pastor Grayling E. Ferrand

You may send your correspondence and tax-deductible contributions to:
Reaching Across the World Ministries, Inc.
PO Box 60254
Brooklyn, New York 11206
Pastor_Ferrand@rawministries.org

Preface

It may appear at times throughout this book that the author is angry. The truth is that sometimes anger is appropriate. However, it is believed, that the anger I experienced was a natural response to external conditions, rather than learned behavior.

The author appeals to his readers to keep an open mind and to try to understand that the way the author felt in 1970 is not necessarily the way he feels now in 2002. Not only do we sometimes fall and get up, we also learn from our experiences, and we change.

As times have changed and followed a certain course, so too has the author in his experiences. A person's past behavior is a reflection of his or her consciousness back then; it does not tell you who the person is today or their future. Pastor Ferrand has gone through a transformation much like the Word of God speaks of: being "transformed by the renewing of your mind." If you really want to know about a person, ask him and more than likely he will tell you.

It is hoped that this transformation will be seen as the author's life unfolds in the pages of this book. I do not profess to be better than any of my other brothers and sisters who have equal potential. I hope and pray for those people who have not reached deep within themselves to extract this potential and reach for their goals as I am reaching for mine.

It was on March 9, 1994 when the idea struck me to write an autobiography; I had to write a short one for a sociology class in was taking while I was incarcerated. I distinctly remember that although I was not a typist, I typed as if I had done so for years. It was as if I was not typing myself. Before I knew it, I had finished at least 50 pages, which I have not changed. It was as if something or someone (God) was doing the typing. After completing the assignment for the sociology class, I realized that there might be some potential for an autobiography.

Roger Bands, a friend of mine, asked me why I was writing an autobiography for a sociology class, when sociology is primarily the study of social groups. I told him, "It's what the teacher asked for. Maybe he wants to take excerpts from the class' autobiographies and write a book because these people are always studying prisoners."

There are certain sociological and psychological factors that condition and program our behaviors and our gut-level values and feelings about life and things in general. I have attempted to identify and incorporate these components in this book.

Thanks to my younger brother Nike, who is writing a book called *The Making of Men*, I was inspired to complete this book. In addition, I need to pay for my master's degree and PhD, as well as my wife's bachelors and masters degrees, and the CSW (Certified Social Worker) she is pursuing now. The Bible says that your gifts will make a way for you and I believe that God will work this out, for he has not given us a spirit of bondage, nor does he want us to remain in bondage. That is why we fall down, but we get back up.

I have tried to be as real as real can get. I have attempted to show how sociology, psychology, and other sciences relate to the everyday lives of many in our society, but in sort of a down-to-earth version.

Herein is a story of crime, poverty, tragedy, and transformation. I have written about the effects of slavery, heroin, burglary, coke, reefer, guns, courts, injustice, unwritten justice, and change. There is no holding back on truth and no limit to what God can do. I have faith in God for an appearance on the Oprah Winfrey show, a play deal, and a movie deal with Spike Lee so that the school loans can be paid for.

TABLE OF CONTENTS

TABLE OF CONTENTS

Forward

Pastor Grayling E. Ferrand is a dreamer living in the new millennium with great hopes of creating social changes that will enhance the quality of life for those less fortunate throughout the world. His first step in attempting to make this dream a reality is to secure his PhD in Human Services with a Specialization in Managing Non-profit Organizations. Oh yes, he is a man with a strategic plan who constantly seeks direction from God the Master Planner, and His Holy Ghost.

Pastor Ferrand believes his plan is God's plan for his life. He seeks to assist in the uplifting of fallen humanity by reaching across the world and ministering to the masses, helping them to get organized, galvanized and prepared for the next generation. He wants them to know that with God they can get up!

Pastor Ferrand does not take credit for any good he may do; instead, he gives all the honor and glory to God. He seeks to continue developing and designing constructive actions geared toward helping to empower individuals on all levels of their existence. He is one of the founders of "Reaching Across the World Ministries, Inc.," a Pentecostal not-for-profit 501c(3) tax-exempt organization. RAW Ministries' mission is to "Uplift Humanity, One Soul at a Time" by conducting needs assessments, and developing research methods, plans of action, implementation strategies, and evaluative tools to help measure and determine the reliability and validity of the program initiatives.

Pastor Ferrand has begun to network with people to establish links among individuals and organizations in an effort to collaborate. He has begun to use today's technology, such as the Internet, to communicate the vision and share the good news across the world. He seeks to feed those that are hungry, cloth the naked, and help those who are caught in webs of confusion in mental or physical prisons. He further seeks to provide counseling to the chemically dependent, those who suffer from domestic violence, those who struggle with their sexual identities, and those in need of anger management, parenting classes, bereavement groups, and marriage counseling. He seeks to speak internationally to the depressed and shut-in or shutout, and those suffering from other strongholds. Most of all, he would like to assist people in becoming empowered on the natural level and minister to them about God in hopes that they may go before the altar of God and accept Jesus Christ as their Personal Lord and Savior, so they may receive salvation and be delivered from those things that are not of God.

Pastor Ferrand's concerns have led him to speak in prisons, churches, colleges, and at family and social gatherings. He presently instructs a weekly bible class where he teaches and preaches the words and deeds of the Lord. He has been on talk shows such as Judge Hatchett and has spoken in youth programs. He does not just "talk the talk" but he is "walking the walk."

Pastor Ferrand presently is pursuing a PhD in Human Services with a Specialization in Managing Non-profit Agencies at Capella University. As a result of his numerous credentials and his pursuit of a doctorate, many people might say he is on his way. However, despite the fact that his desires may be noble, his present works good and his intentions commendable, it must be told that Pastor Ferrand was not always so focused and positive. There was a time when he fell down but through the grace and mercy of God Almighty he's gotten back up! Hallelujah, Praise God.

Prologue

He is an ex-prisoner
He is an ex-crack addict
He is an ex-pimp
He is an ex-homeless beggar
He is an ex-angel dust smoker
He is an ex-alcohol drinker
He is an ex-heroin shooter
He is an ex-cocaine sniffer
He is an ex-LSD, ex-acid pill dropper
He is an ex-gang member
He is a sexual abuse survivor
He is Pastor Grayling E. Ferrand, The Prodigal Son.

Up from the muck and the mire, saved, sanctified, and filled with the Holy Ghost. He is a man transformed by the renewing of his mind, heart and spirit. He is a new creature, old things are passed away and behold all things are new. He is a man after God's own heart, a man with his finger on the pulse of communities in crisis. He has been *raised* up to understand many of the social and cultural ills that exist in today's society. He is a man with a vision, shaped and molded for times such as these. He envisions a new and improved social, cultural, economical and political movement within and amongst humanity. The transformation process begins by doing some introspection and retrospection. After all is said and done, he wants you to know: "I fell down, but with God's help I got up!"

This autobiography challenges the law student to come to grips with the reality that our judicial system is not flawless but rather it can be racist, discriminatory, and sometimes seemingly cynical in its plans, actions and implementation regarding the law. Do not get it wrong, the author loves being an African-American; however, due to his being on the other side of the fence there are some things that he wishes to impart concerning the judicial system which have affected his life forever. This story challenges the schools of higher learning that talk about sociology, psychology, criminology and cultural diversity (i.e., alternative life styles), chemical dependency and their affects on the many African-American men in contemporary society.

It is suggested that this book be used to ask these questions in school: how do the experiences discussed herein relate to the lives of the scholars, and how do these experiences fit in with textbook knowledge. In doing so you will be contributing to a great cause right here in America *and* abroad.

Feel free to analyze, compare and synthesize the information. It is hoped that using this book as a text in schools will act as an intervention for some learners who may be searching for light. It is my hope and belief that directly or indirectly due to this book many will be enlightened, inspired, motivated, encouraged, and will receive salvation. If knowledge is obtained in degrees, then I pray that some degree of knowledge be imparted to each and every reader.

The Conception

It was December 1993 and it was cold outside. There were no trees to see, no children crying, or the smell of a newborn baby with its mother's milk around its neck. In fact, there were no baby bottles, bibs or pampers.

No. Instead, there were just the steel bars, the concrete walls, and echoes of tough-grown gangsters crying all the time on the telephone. I had seen a brother stabbed or cut with razors from one side of his face to the other because he used the phone. All he wanted was a few dollars for cigarettes, some sneakers, and a visit. Who knows though, perhaps he didn't get his pimp's dope as was demanded of him. If you asked him he could not tell you why the other guy stabbed him. Guys like him were sent to either involuntary protective custody or placed under tighter security. It was not hard to conceive this story in jail, where the birds never fly but sing all types of songs like the blues, unless you like pain, dehumanization, deprivation and denial of heterosexual relationships.

Like almost two million others in the United States, I was caught up in the criminal justice system. I was incarcerated for a crime that was never committed. I was innocent and my soul felt like Joseph who was thrown down the well. I was angry, I was sad, I was sometimes confused, and I cried easily when I thought of what they had done to me. I was stripped of my freedom, had been taken away from my family and thrown into a hostile environment like Daniel in the lions' den. I was asking the Lord to help me, because I could see no justice in the system.

Nevertheless, despite being incarcerated unjustly, I began writing this book. I did not exactly know why. I figured it was better than getting stabbed in the Clinton yard and having dirt kicked in my face by my so-called homeboys. When the wrath comes, people move.

I was attending my fourth year at Marist College as a psychology major. I had made the Dean's List with first honors. During my scholastic endeavors I had studied some literature along with other subjects (i.e., core requirements and electives). An attempt was being made to incorporate these things into an autobiography.

From dropout to the Dean's List: ironically, in some mysterious way, perhaps there is a master plan of justice that I do not understand.

Lost Roots

My family background is important to know in order to understand me. Being aware of our past can help us better understand the why and how of the present. It should also help us to prevent repeating those things that are detrimental or destructive.

As far as I can remember, my roots begin with my mother. My mother was a girl from the ghetto. She was born in 1942 in a town called Port smith, Virginia. Shortly after her birth she somehow ended up in a garbage can. She was discovered amongst the muck, mire, and garbage, a jewel cast amongst the swine. Thank God for the sanitation worker who found her there in a box, in the rainy wee hours of the morning. A white man named Charlie Ferrand, who married a black woman named Queeny, later adopted her. My mother received the name Gloria Ferrand and was given the approximate birth date of August 2, 1942. The actual circumstances surrounding how my mother ended up in the garbage can will probably never be known. Perhaps her mother was an alcoholic, perhaps an innocent little girl who had been violated, God only knows. Mommy never seemed to like to discuss the circumstances surrounding her birth and adoption. The fact of the matter is that the devil meant it for evil, but God turned it around for good.

As a result of the mystery of my mother's family origins, I often wonder: who are my uncles and aunts on her side of the family? Are there any cousins? If I could just see one of my grandparents' face and touch the hem of his or her garment. Perhaps it is just wishful thinking and my spirit stirs for no reason. Lineages cannot only be important in the history of the kings and queens of biblical times and Europe. For me, time would pass and these things would become repressed and perhaps at times expressed in acts of stupidity or frustration. WHO IS MY FAMILY? IT'S JUST NOT FAIR!!! I can imagine how the slaves felt when their children were stripped from their mothers' wombs. Different scenario, same end. That's deep, deep psychological stuff, yet not deep enough to warrant reparations. I heard one person say we don't owe you one red cent. But that is another story.

My mother didn't like to discuss my biological father or how they met. One day when I was about 12 years old I asked her, "Mommy, who is my real father?" My mother looked at me in amazement, and I returned the same look. This question was asked out of instinct and nothing else because no one had ever told me that the man who had raised me wasn't my biological father. To this day I do not know why I even asked the question with no precursor.

I remember the answer that my mother gave me. She told me that my father had come from an island; his name was Luther LeGair (nicknamed Pepe), that he needed a green card for citizenship, and he married the girl across the street because my mother did not marry him fast enough. Little did he know, my mother was pregnant. Shortly thereafter, while working on a ship he died as a result of a freak accident; a light beam fell on him and crushed him. He was survived by a daughter (Lisa), and me, a bastard son he never knew he had. I hope he got his green card.

It is unfortunate that my biological dad and I never met. Like the circumstances surrounding my mother's birth, I was again unable to know who my paternal grandmother and grandfather were. The fact is that I never met any of my grandparents. I also never met any of my cousins, uncles or aunts. No, not one. My spirit sometimes wonders: Who are they? Where are they?

Perhaps yearning to know and find the missing pieces has in some way contributed to the shaping and the molding of my personality and character. I have always felt cheated in life, hurt, unloved, and have had a sense of incongruence, so to speak. The question of the whereabouts of my family members is always alive in my mind, in my veins, and in the deepness of my soul, locked in there forever.

Grayling

"Push! Breathe. Push! Breathe. Push! It's coming, you've got it. Therrre we go!" The doctor slapped me on the buttocks and the sound of a child's cry spouted sporadically through the air as the newborn's mangled mouth kept screaming and yelling as if he wanted to say something. Was this baby mad from birth? It didn't matter how much I yelled and screamed for I was in the world now, a world that is not always fair, and sometimes wicked and strange, where the living dead rule the day and night.

The doctor said cordially, in a professional tone, "You have a healthy 6 lb. 10 oz. boy, Ma'am." After the healing of the stitches, my mother Gloria went home, now with two children and no father for either of them (at the time, my mother already had a 13-month-old girl by Pepe). When she got home with the new baby her mother told her, "That baby will never be anything" and questioned whether I was a legitimate offspring of my step-grandfather. My mother says that she never felt more insulted in her life; she kept this information for 40 years before telling me. It's all good, though. I must have come out my mother with my spirit yearning to know where the missing pieces of my heart were, the family I never knew.

So, on May 18, 1960 (under the zodiac sign of the bull), I, Grayling E. Ferrand, was born at Saint Luke's Hospital in New York. People were selling drugs and talking about revolution, singing and shouting words like: "Say it loud. I'm black and I'm proud." "Power to the people!", "The people is the power and the power is the people!", "Un-Gow-Wer, black power!", "The white man is the devil and the black man is god!"

Bubba

Bubba, my (common-law) stepfather, raised me. My mother used to look out of the window at 126 W. 115ᵗʰ Street and listen to Bubba and the guys playing steel pan music. One day, Bubba spotted her and told her that she was going to be his girl. He came to dinner later, and he never left.

Bubba came here from Trinidad. He was almost crushed to death on a boat when coming over. He was a smooth guy, with that Trinidadian accent. Clean cut and no spring chicken, he had several children in Trinidad. I never asked Bubba why he left and came to America or the circumstances that caused him to abandon the family there. My mother and Bubba would have five sons together. Today, the children of the former relationship know their siblings, cousins, aunts, etc in America.

I was the oldest male and I was going to look out for my brothers and sister if ever the time came. But when I was growing up, Bubba was the knight in shining armor. He was responsible for his five children and two that weren't his. I commend him for that.

Reflections

Going back as far as I can go, I find myself in the early sixties. It was around 1966 because I was in public school. My teacher told me that I was good in artwork. I did not like the teacher, perhaps because she was white, although my step-grandfather was white too. But to me it was different. My step-grandfather was the "nice white" because I knew him and I could go to Lee's Department Store on 125th Street and get a quarter from him. The teacher was the kind of white that the Black Muslims and the Nation of Gods and Earths were talking about, the ones that smiled in your face and told lies, right? At least, that is what I must have thought subconsciously because even though she was very nice to me I don't know why I did not like her. Perhaps John Locke was right when he talked about people being born with a clean slate. Maybe all of this "black man, white man" stuff was confusing me. In fact, at this time I don't think I liked any white people except my step-grandfather. I wasn't sure why.

Another vision comes to mind: it was when my little brother, Leonard, was born. I remember my mother coming home from the hospital and there were some grapes being brought with the new baby. These grapes were green and I still remember because, I guess, I wanted some so bad. I made a pig of myself when I got them. I forgot all about the new baby once those sweet/sour green grapes were in my mouth. I could not have been any older than five then because I am about five years older than Leonard. I don't remember when my mother was pregnant with my other brothers or when she came home with them. I don't know if this is due to the drugs I later used in life, which I intend to speak more about later.

I can also remember one of the first fights that I had. I was scared as hell because everyone was talking about the toughness of my opponent, plus I don't think that my father taught me how to fight. I would learn this later in life in prison, although I never developed the heart or nerve to be a violent person and a fighter. There are those who would disagree with me, and, in fact, consider me very violent. I think I have acted violently in situations and reacted violently due to circumstances, but I don't consider this being a violent person. I was faced with situations that called for me either to take flight or stand and fight. I have always felt my spirit to be humble like a rabbit's; however, if a rabbit is pushed into a corner it can become violent.

People who have developed a violent heart may be blessed I guess, but I, for one, don't see myself as having been so. Maybe I am a little modest in my evaluation or maybe I am understating myself; nevertheless, I would rather just say that the potential for both violence and non-violence exists, and I just hope and pray that when needed either one will kick in and serve its purpose.

Unfortunately, later on in my life Probation labeled me as someone who is very violent, in need of help, and in a state of denial, although they didn't tell me straight out what I was denying. The last probation report stated that I was maladaptive, psychopathic, and antisocial, but competent enough to stand trial (of course) and to be sentenced as if I possessed good sense. Sometimes I do not think half of those probation and pre-sentencing counselors know what they are talking about. I literally cried because I was so hurt that I had been found guilty for something I did not do. I told the pre-sentencing counselor exactly what had happened. He interpreted the truth as a lie and accused me of being in denial.

My stepfather made me fight once and I received a busted nose. Bubba then made me fight some more. I guess he felt that by letting me get my behind kicked some more, it would enable me to win against someone that I just didn't seem to be able to beat. Maybe I could have beaten the guy, if I would not have been forced to fight. I never liked being told what to do. I guess this started when I reached the stage of the terrible twos, saying, "No! No! Mines!"

For a guy who supposedly couldn't read well my stepfather read the newspapers all the time (unless he was just looking at the pictures). He watched the amazing Mets and those Knickerbockers. He was a small guy, but he had a lot of guts. I saw him stand up to this big giant one time when we were going through the turnstile in Manhattan. The guy had said something to my mother, I believe, because my mother was bowlegged (they called her a cowgirl). Anyway, my stepfather started going off and talking loud with that Trinidadian accent and temperament. My mother pleaded with him to take it easy and she probably thought she was saving him, but I don't think so. Basically, Bubba didn't take any s--t.

I remember he used to beat the alphabets into my little brother Adam, so I made sure to learn mine. My mother used to try to plead with my pops and make him understand that you could not beat learning into someone. He was serious about education; I think that is the main reason every one of my brothers and my sister can read, write, and count.

Sexual Deviance

I don't remember at exactly what age my brothers and I indulged in experimenting with our genitals; I only remember that I was in elementary school and I was being influenced from the outside. The first encounter was with an adult who lured me into a basement as a child. I remember being molested while I was down there and being forced to allow him to perform oral sex on me. Obviously, he was an individual possessed by a lustful pedophile spirit. For decades I felt bad that I had even allowed myself to be duped into indulging in this type of behavior. I saw homosexuals coming out of the closet with this new hippie phase, and we all lived in the "Yellow Submarine" mentality. Why look to the Scriptures when we had Elijah Muhammad and the black man being called God?

I do not understand the full impact that being molested as a child had on my sexually-deviant behavior. Although some say that boys will be boys, I can't help but feel responsible for my ignorant acts. I was very curious about how the sex thing worked and being molested did not help me to have the normal child-like curiosity. I do not know exactly where it all came from; however, it took some time before I could learn to forgive myself for the things that happened to me. Yet, if I am going to tell the story and keep it real in hopes of somebody coming out of such situations, than so be it.

I think Butchy was the strongest influence in getting me involved with this behavior. He was a blond white boy passing for Puerto Rican. He was very mischievous and he could fight, so most guys did not mess with him. He and I hung out together. One day he asked me to come with him to the aqueduct in the Bronx. When we got there he asked me if I had ever seen cum. I told him that I didn't. He then told me that he was going to have this guy make him cum. As we continued to walk and talk, I really did not understand what he exactly had in mind. All of a sudden there was this other guy who was a little younger than us there. Butchy made this kid give him a blowjob while I watched. This was the first time I had ever seen something like this. I do not know if Butchy had been molested as a child or where he had picked up that behavior.

In my mind, I was amazed and I didn't pay much attention to anything else. I didn't know whether or not this was a regular thing and I didn't ask. In retrospect, I see that this was the beginning of deviant behavior and the beginning of negative influences. It may be difficult for some to handle, my discussing this. However, the reality is that children are discussing these things in elementary schools. We cannot act as though there is no elephant in the room when there is. We cannot act as though HIV/AIDS only affects gay and lesbian people. We must remove the blinders and deal head-on with the enemy that hides behind the cover of fear, lies, deceit, and cowardice. The point is that children are curious at this age and are persuaded by negative influences, so we must watch as well as pray. I wonder, as we sometimes try to hide these realities in society, how many little boys and girls are being molested and we are oblivious of it. With the onslaught of multi-cultural curricula and tolerance for other lifestyles, what used to be deviant behavior is quickly becoming the norm.

I realize now that my little brothers were depending on me to lead them because they trusted me as their older brother. Perhaps some of them now do not really see me in a positive light or look up to me. I can't blame them. Maybe I'm searching for a defense mechanism or someone to blame. Who wouldn't? Unlike the twelve-step program that suggests a person make amends with the wrongs they have done, I can't see myself telling my brothers that I am sorry for what I have done. I have done so before, either directly or indirectly, but it never seems to be enough because it doesn't undo what has been done. Furthermore, it may do more harm than good.

I often wonder what type of psychological effects may have come out of all those acts, and I search for who is really to blame. This foul, corrupted, and inhumane society often comes to mind, a spill over from the ancient Greeks with their warped thinking and sexually-deviant behavior. Today, I realize that it is the same old spirit that tempted Eve, the same spirit that tempted Jesus for 40 days and nights. Satan and his demonic imps are the spirits that need to be bound up, and those who have been snared by his traps and pitfalls need to be delivered. Thank God for deliverance.

Two things I learned from the above: 1) a parent can be doing all the right things inside the home but they must be very aware of the influences that other children may have on their children and be watchful of their children's friends' behavior because what the other children may have experienced in their households (sexual abuse, etc.) or their immediate social environment may spill over into other homes. I do not say this to suggest people become paranoid, but rather aware, and 2) we are taught to take advantage of people in this society as opposed to helping them or being concerned with their true plight. This is why we can have our businesses move to third world countries in the name of capitalism. Capitalism supports the notion of "me first"; that's why people needed to fight for civil rights. Some people believe that they have the right to take advantage of people because they perceive themselves as special and the other people as not being special. If I had to say a word about homosexuality and other such behaviors, I would first and foremost be careful to say that I am not judging anyone. However, based on my experience, I would say that this is a strong spirit that only God can deliver someone from, and no matter how far gone we think we may be, God is able to deliver us.

Triggering Trauma

I can remember learning about slavery in the fourth grade; I believe it was during Black History week. I can distinctly remember that the teacher showed us some pictures in a textbook. One of the pictures was of a black person who had been nailed to a cross, burned, and lynched. Also in the picture was a bunch of white people with liquor bottles and beer in their hands, standing around this poor corpse. They and their children had smiles on their little white faces as if they were enjoying a feast. At the time I didn't realize the psychodynamic effects that this picture would have on me. I know that I was very emotionally disturbed about what I was seeing. Deep down inside I began to dislike and hate the people who were responsible for this. The teacher just said, "This, children, is what happened to your people during slavery." I was saying to myself, "This is too much for me." I don't know if teachers are aware that some children are able to pick up and identify with these types of pictures and to empathize with what they are being shown. From that moment on, I would never be the same.

This inflamed me and helped to give credence to what the freedom fighters were saying. Movements like the Black Panthers influenced me, so I'd draw black power fists and people with Afros in class. I even wore an Afro, although later I would get a perm or use a hot comb to make it appear as if I had so-called good hair. Today, it is possible that as a result of all of those perms and hot combs I am now bald. I had heard of the B.L.A. (Black Liberation Army), The Black Muslims, Martin Luther King Jr., and especially Malcolm X, whose type of spirit I could feel. Yes! Malcolm X. This was the response needed for those wicked people in the picture. At that time we had songs on the airwaves screaming, "Say it loud! I'm black and I'm proud", "To be young, gifted and black!" and the spirit of freedom against racial discrimination was in the air. Seeing this picture was a turning point for me.

Ink Spot

Despite the fact that it was an era in which black people were trying to gain back the self-respect and self-esteem that they had been stripped of, I found myself subconsciously brainwashed and had an inferiority complex. When I was very little I walked to 125th Street to Lee's Department Store where my step-grandfather worked, just to get a few cents. But it was a white man giving it to me.

At home I watched sambo's, jiggaboo's, and pickaninnies and thought they were funny. The cartoons like Bugs Bunny portrayed Africans as cannibals, always getting ready to eat people. J.J. Evans of "Good Times" reminded me of home. The pictures of Jesus in church were all white and Mommy always called on Jesus when she was sick.

At school my friends and I would never have admitted to dating or going with any dark-skinned girl. Someone would ask in a peculiar way, "Yo, you go with that black spook, that ink spot?" "Hell No!" would be the reply, even if one of us did. You couldn't get me to claim a dark-skinned girl. I was tricked into believing light, bright or damn-near white was always right. This was the attitude of those in my peer group at that time. Despite all the black talk going around then, something was embedded in our psychological makeup. It would be a long time before I really learned that there was nothing wrong with being black or loving blackness.

At this time I was pretty good in my studies. In fact, I was being considered for a special school. However, I was getting bigger, wiser, tougher, and more popular. I became bad in school and got into a lot of trouble. I was suspended. I hung out with the tough guys, and we did everything under the sun and many of those things were stupid. We robbed all the white boys at P.S. 86 in the Bronx off Kingsbridge Road, with the exception of one white kid who fought like a Spartan. One time,

Don Jones, Don Smith and I were on the school staircase, cutting and looking for something to do. Along came this kid and Don Jones put pressure on the kid to perform oral sex on us.

Hitting

I began smoking cigarettes at about ten years old, as well as reefer. I also used to do what we called "hitting". Hitting was when you stole things from the store and sold them for money. I stole roach spray, Goya olive oil, meats (bacon, steak, ham), coffee, and batteries. We also stole things like baby clothing, sneakers; material for tailor-made pants, and anything else we could sell. I could make about $100 a day just hitting. My stepfather was giving me about 50 cents a week as an allowance. He may have meant well but this was really a joke when I looked at what the other guys were making from hitting, which is what led me to learn how to hit from a guy named Carlos Dent. I don't think that Carlos' family gave him an allowance and so he learned how to steal instead. This was a skill that many other children learned from him. I say skill because he could steal things right before your eyes, if you just blinked. He could steal so many items and you would not even know it until he began unloading for a buyer. He could walk through three aisles in a grocery store and from each isle he would place in his possession about three items. He would have two bottles of olive oil in the front of his pants under the shirt, some steak in the back of his pants, some batteries in his socks, some coffee down the sleeves of his jacket, and probably something else somewhere. I too learned how to be a thief like this, although not as good as the "teacher", which is what we all called Carlos concerning this skill.

Bright Boy

I was proud of the fact that I could do algebra as early as the sixth grade. People wonder what happened to the young great minds that used to show so much promise; there are different factors for different individuals. To understand, I think these are some of the things that need to be considered: If a person can be traumatized by being forced to watch certain atrocities being committed against a loved one, it's also possible for a child to be traumatized by seeing and identifying with particular atrocities in pictures. Whether or not such a thing can trigger some psychological suppression of trauma is debatable and subjective. The main thing is that when someone has just suffered a traumatic experience, someone should try to get that person some professional help. However, when we consider the many traumatic experiences that black people have been forced to endure, we also find that there has been no real debriefing or professional help given to them.

I mention this because I am black and I think that what I believe I am, or who I believe I am, has a lot to do with the history of my family as it relates to socio-cultural experiences, etc. I don't believe that all of the effects of slavery on the psychological, spiritual, economical, physical, biological, and social levels have been clearly defined and fully understood. Therefore, I choose not to rule out any possibilities of slavery's effects on me.

Party Time

I began to hang out a lot as my mother moved from the Bronx to Manhattan and Manhattan to the Bronx. I learned about traveling by trains early, so it was no problem for me when I decided to hang out. I used to go to a place called Chuck Center on E.115th St. or to the Foster Projects where we did break dancing as early as 1971/1972. I was a very good dancer, and I would draw a crowd wherever and whenever I danced. The same way people would battle to see who played music the best and scratched records the best is the same way good dancers were evaluated. They would get things like, "Ohh! Oh s--t! Do that s--t, do that s--t." Mostly the fellows challenged the fellows, and every now and then you would have partners who rehearsed some steps and battled other partners, or they just danced for the people to show their talent. I had a partner named David and we would practice all week instead of doing homework. When we went to a party we tore the floor up and any other partners that wanted to battle. If we had someone who wanted to go heads up, David would ask me, "You want to get, or me?" We were confident in our ability to get busy. I cannot forget that there were quite a few girls who battled on the dance floor, too. As a boy you had to be good to battle a female dancer because it was terrible to let a female dancer out dance you with slicker moves. How could you face the crew after they have stood there and watched her dance circles around you, which is something that they literally did, almost like a war dance. They would stomp around in a circle until they sort of heated up, and then they would dive to the floor from numerous positions and do some things down there and come up from there in numerous positions. The going down and coming up were the good parts of the dance, although they could do some wicked stuff while standing and dancing.

I used to go uptown to the Twilight Zone, the Heave low, and wherever there were parties. Back then Cool Herk was the man on the wheels, straight up with no chaser. He took the place of your Eric B and Rakim of today, but he just played the music.

Slow music and grinding with the girls was also the in thing. Even if you'd worked up a sweat you could dance with a girl to a slow jam with no offense. If she liked you it didn't matter anyway because she had you in her arms, between her legs, where she wanted you.

House parties were common where people gave parties in their house to earn money. They sold chicken, beer, and other food, charging 25 to 50 cents at the door. There was very little violence then, if any. I don't know what happened to those days where we had centers open for recreation, parties, etc. I don't know what happened to the closeness we exhibited toward one another more often than not. They just seem to have vanished with the change of political representatives.

While hanging out I learned other means to obtain money. For example, I learned to soup tokens out of the turnstiles. I would get a few tokens to buy a joint if I didn't feel like going into a store to hit. Basically, I was beginning to feel like nothing really mattered but making or getting money. I guess this is one of the reasons why our youth of today don't care whether or not they have to kill someone to get a jacket. We paved the way for this type of behavior and, realistically speaking, to me they have only become a little more ruthless. Our society says, "Get yours!" Capitalism, how sweet it is! Bulls--t! How dangerous it is, is more like it. How much do we really lose for the price of gold or silver? What does it profit us to gain worldly possessions but to lose our souls?

Curt

At one point I even participated in having sexual intercourse with a homosexual in the community. His name was Curt and we all called him Pol. He would have fried chicken cooking all the time with lots of spices and seasonings, just the way black boys liked it. There was lots of hot boiling rice, candied yams, and large ice-cold cokes. The aroma would lure impoverished black male youth into its stewed web of deception. I tell you, it's a crime to be poor. He would also have a lot of dresses that he got from the garment district. He would ask the children who didn't have that much but hung out around the way if they wanted to sell some dresses and they could have 1/3 of the money. He probably stole the dresses to make a profit, but the scheme appears to have been to get all the boys up into his apartment to try to get them to f--k him; and f--ked he was by a lot of the boys. For example: Bones, J.J., Carlos, Jimmy, Darrel, Dave, Don, and the list goes on.

He'd buy guys sweaters, shoes, and other things and say things like: "This is my man, whatever he says goes." If you wanted some of the food he was cooking, he would say, "Ask Don!" if he was letting Don f--k him at the time. Later, if Don wasn't there, he might give you something to eat and after fattening you up for the kill he would say, "I want some of that d--k." The old bastard sucked the life out of many minors. I'll say this: a poor child is more vulnerable to a pervert with a lollipop.

Meanwhile, as I was learning these things, my mother was trying to be a good provider. She often left my stepfather because he was a little abusive in expressing his point at times. There were other things going on, but that is Gloria's autobiography. There were times when my siblings and I would get butter knives (especially my sister Elaine) when our stepfather was beating our mother. We would cry and threaten to run with a knife to the rescue, but this took a lot of heart, which none of us had developed enough of yet, or we just had good sense. I guess we were all saying to each other, "I am not going up against that big bad gorilla."

Hey, Mamma's Got It Good

Mother attempted to provide for us by selling drugs. She couldn't read and write as well as she would have liked to. My mother also didn't have a high school diploma, but she stressed the importance of obtaining one to her children.

When the drug addicts were in a hurry to get more drugs, sometimes my mother would rush to get the cocaine cut and on the streets to the anxiously waiting customers. I was young, cunning, and enthusiastic. As a result, I would con my mother, saying, "Mommy, I'll clean up for you 'cause I see you're busy." She'd say, "How thoughtful. Thank you, son," and she'd leave. Unfortunately, I was too fast. I noticed the way the drug was administered via the nasal passage. I used to volunteer to clean off the mirror every time my mother was trying to get things together. I guess because I was the oldest boy and so cunning, my mother never really thought anything of it. How would she know that I would scrape off the residue of the coke and place it into some aluminum foil and stash it? In her mind she was selling drugs because she had to, so I wouldn't have to. Hence, I was sniffing cocaine as young as about twelve years old, and plenty of it, if and when I wanted to. I used to give some away to my friends because I felt like a big shot that way. One guy might bring me a joint and say, "Yo, man! I have some weed." I would say, "Oh yeah? I have some coke, homeboy!" That was like when the white kids say, "Wow! That's really cool, man! Like, far out dude!"

Gloria made sure that she bought her children the finer things in life. We wore very good shoes, pants, shirts, and sweaters. In addition, we ate steak and good food every night while she was hustling. We went to school without a worry of what we would eat. In fact, while she was out hustling there was always plenty of food in the freezer. Because of her, we learned to cook and to make our beds, sew, etc. I guess Mommy wanted her boys to not have to depend on a woman for anything but reproduction. And she didn't want them to have to do what she was doing. I understand that now.

I think it's also important to mention here that I was also very creative. I knew how to fix things like old radios or TV's. I would pick something out of the garbage and fix it, although I had no schooling for this trade. I would figure out basic things like noticing a bulb was broken in a TV. I would stack that TV until I found another one and take the tube out of it and place it into the first TV. I also noticed when a wire had popped off of something it should be attached to, and I would attach it. More often than not, that was the problem.

Survival Skills

I eventually began to sell drugs. First it was reefer; I would sell loose joints for a dollar. You could get a bag of reefer that could make you ten joints. The bag would cost $5 and therefore I could make a 100% profit. I received my first half-ounce by stealing and selling Slim's gold bracelets. Slim was our guardian when my mother went to serve time in jail for cocaine charges. This was probably the first sign of addiction, or being rendered powerless over the things in my environment. It was not like me to feel compelled to steal from family or people I loved. I remember this moment as if it was happening now, and I know that I really felt remorseful and shameful when I stole the bracelets. Eventually I would learn the tricks of the trade: I could mix a little tea with the reefer or make the joints a little skinnier to stretch the profits, or sell to white people for twice the price. From loose joints I moved on to sell bags of reefer and make more than 200% profit between bags and joints.

Before selling reefer I had learned to pack bags, shine shoes, and carry groceries from the supermarket for people. I just about learned to do it all. I snatched pocketbooks, stole from stores, snatched products off of trucks, sold drugs, and got high on the drugs that I sold. I was still in school while doing all of this. I did not have any problem keeping up with the schoolwork because it didn't seem like there was any work to keep up with. Furthermore, I was very bright but school wasn't holding my attention as much as the streets were. Even now in college I don't really have the interest or attention I would like.

In junior high school I pretty much roamed the hallways with the girls, necking on the staircase. I wanted to test my skills with the girls and plus my mother kept me looking good for them, so what the hell. It was when I went to high school that I noticed there was a popular demand for drugs, and angel dust was the thing that happened to come out. This drug set black people back 20 years or more.

Much Better

I happened to live right where angel dust came out (what a coincidence?), which was right around 112th Street in the Foster Projects. I started to sell angel dust and smoke it as well. Many people wonder how I ever bounced back from this. I still wonder what the long-term effects of this devastating drug will be. There was Crazy Eddie, Jack and Jill, Do, Jack, Reverend Ike, Coma, Busy Bee, and especially Much Better. All of these were names of angel dust.

This was a period in my life that was very trying for me because I was out there on my own; I believe I had an apartment at the age of fifteen. I was selling angel dust and smoking it; I smoked almost fifteen bags a day. My stepfather came up to the Bronx to look for me as I had lost a tremendous amount of weight (I was already small boned). Eventually my mother moved to Baltimore, Maryland, which is how I believe I was saved from going insane from the drugs. I was very lucky to have come back from that drug trip when many of my brothers and sisters have never recovered. It is a shame that so many good families were destroyed because of this drug and others. Somehow we must learn to change the cycle of destruction that drugs have caused and continue to cause. The Alcohol and Substance Abuse Treatment (A.S.A.T.) programs and other therapeutic programs are good but they have proved to be not good enough. I believe that the real solutions will come from the brothers inside of the prisons or from those that are released. I don't say this because I was a prisoner, but rather this is a gut-level feeling of mine. I myself intend to do what I can to help in changing the tide of things for black people involved with the use and sale of drugs. In addition, I will help in other areas of the struggle if and when I am able to do so.

Stack 'em Shake

Around this time I played a lot of 21 Blackjack, as I had learned early on how to gamble at many games. Around the age of twelve I was able to stack in a matter of seconds for at least four or five people playing poker. It was something that a keen eye would pick up on after losing all the money you had made from stealing for weeks.

They called me "Shaky Shake and Bake," "Shaky Shake," "Shake," or mostly just "Shaky". I got this name while in elementary school. Don Smith and I were teasing some girls and telling them that our penis's wanted them. At first I was going to call mine Rover but I didn't really like that name, so I chose Shake. I always tell people when they ask me, "Where did you get that nickname?" "Oh! I got it from people who use to watch me play basketball." I used to shake people so bad that they would say, "Shake him, Shaky", or "Shake 'em, bake 'em and take 'em."

Gambling was another way to earn fast money. After a while it wasn't just earning or getting money that mattered to me, it was getting it fast. We called it "fast money" or a "quick buck". Who cared about "easy come, easy go"? That was just saying that it was easy to get more, so what the f--k! And got more is what I did.

In addition to getting the money fast, the way in which one got his money fast was just as important. It was comparable to a doctor with a PhD making money and his assistant making money only because the doctor allowed him to. Well, the stickup kid was like the doctor with the PhD; he was the boss of his own destiny, or so it would seem. The drug dealer was another one who was respected for how he earned his money, basically because he was making fast money and the amount was important. There was no real comparison between the guy working in

McDonald's, the drug dealer, and the man who just robbed your boss, you, and all your co-workers. After all, *Superfly*, *The Mac* and *Black Caesar* were the stars, not the McDonald's waiters. As a result, I developed not necessarily heart, but prestige amongst the fellows. I did whatever I needed to do to get along and be accepted or looked up to. For a 12-year-old to put a gun in someone else's face has nothing to do with heart as much as it has to do with conditioning and programming within his environment.

I learned how to throw Three-Card Molly as a result of an incident that happened when I was about 14 years old. I was sent to the store to buy a couple of goldfish at Blumstein's on 125th St. I had begged my mother for them so much that she gave me $20 to go and buy the fish. All of a sudden, I saw a man throwing three cards: there were two black cards and one red, and they were face cards. He was yelling, "Red! Red! Like a rooster's head. Who had seen the Red? Watch the Red Card. Red! Red! Who seen it just like that?" He sounded like James Brown singing, "Batta Do Tat! Ahing!"

I watched while he and his partners acted as if they were not together. They suckered me in: I said, "Yo, I seen the red!" The man said, "Go ahead, kid, I don't want to take your money." This only made me mad because I was not a kid in my mind, so this was more of an insult than anything else. After watching him throw the cards again, I said in a more demanding voice this time, "Yo! I said I seen the red card." The man said, "O.K. $5 say you didn't." I said, "$20 say I did." "Bet!" said the man. I lost my mother's twenty dollars, went home and told her I lost it in another way. I got three cards and I learned how to throw Three-Card Molly that day. I won way more than $20 in my lifetime from that game and it's still a "vocation" I can use in many societies if I'm down and out.

When we played 21 Blackjack it was about betting big. It was about excitement and dare with most of the crew I grew up with.

Although we were young, we would hit a sting by stickup, sneak thieving, drugs, etc and come to the table where everyone was gambling. The dealer with the "bank" would be shuffling the cards and you would come over and ask, "What's in the bank?" The dealer and everyone else would stop and look at you to see what's up. If the "banker" said $175, everyone would shift from the banker back to you. This was the moment of truth, like the gymnast waiting for his marks. If you asked the question to the man getting the first card, "How much you got of that?" or "Could I stop it up with you?" you were the man, you were down. It didn't matter if you lost that hand or not. You could lose and walk away, but you would still be down and people would be left with the mystery of whether or not you had plenty more and just wanted to share a little of your loot with the homeboys. This was a way of looking out for the brothers. If you won the hand you were the man and you received the bank. Everyone would want to stay in the game because they knew that there was twice as much money in the game as before and maybe they could win it all if their luck kicked in. I have done all of the above on several occasions.

Another game we played with lots of excitement was the game known as "See Low!" which is played with three dice. The banker shoots the dice and if he gets a point between 1 and 6, you must shoot the dice and try to beat his point. If he throws a 1 he loses, and if he throws a 6 he wins. There is a slight difference in the way the bets are placed, though. In 21 Blackjack the banker must know how much you are placing. Not so in See Low! The banker would say, "All money down is a bet and I am paying as far as this money will go." As a result, a line would be formed and you would place your bets under your foot. If the bank was $400 and the first one on the line bet $2 and you were the second man on line and you placed four one-hundred dollar bills inside of a one dollar bill under your foot, you have then placed a bet of $398. If the shooter throws a 1, when he goes to see what he owes you he will find that he owes you the remaining money in his hand and the bank. It is fun to play.

One thing is for sure: A poor kid hustling could come out early in the morning with three dice or a deck of cards and make a bundle of money by the end of the day. He could house a game that would start at 8:00 a.m. and end some 22 hours later. The streets taught me many ways to get mine: there were other games like Chuck-A-Luck, Over-and-Under Lucky Seven, Seven Eleven, etc.

All Alone

My mother was eventually busted for cocaine, and she pleaded guilty as a user. She went to do some time in the Federal Penal System, and I got into a lot of trouble while she was away. My mother was forced to leave her children with a young lady named Slim who was just a child herself. My mother didn't have any family to depend on when things got rough. She always wanted to keep the family together though, which was what she managed to do. However, I would not be such an easy child to look after.

Things were rough. Sometimes I had to steal. I don't say this to persuade the reader to have sympathy for me, but rather to keep things real. I was the oldest of five boys and I had to steal sometimes to make sure that we ate. I would go into the store and place eggs in my pocket and pork chops in my pants as I walked through the aisles. I would throw a pack of bacon and some Pillsbury dough biscuits in my waist. We all liked the cinnamon biscuits, so I usually stole that kind. I guess you can say my earlier skills came in handy during this time.

I fought against the guardian that my mother had chosen for us. I believe that I was really a problem child because even at a young age I was sent to see a psychologist. The problem was that I was trying to express my unhappiness and other feelings that no one seemed to understand.

I threatened Slim one time because she had threatened to beat me with an extension cord. All I could think of was the time that my mother had given my sister a beating with one. I listened and watched this beating take place, and I went to my sister's aid immediately afterward. I had always loved my sister and I still do very much. My sister showed me her wounds when I got close to her. They were atrocious in my opinion; they were different than the normal welts we got from the belt my father used. These wounds were bloodletting, with the letter "u" scribbled all over her young delicate body. Each "u" seemed bigger than it actually was and all appeared to be bleeding. I looked at Slim when she made the threat, and if that didn't give her the message I verbally made it clear that I wasn't having it. I do not remember exactly what I said to her. It must have been something like, "I don't think so! Homey don't play that."

I rebelled against the system and everything around me. I did burglaries, I fought, and I stayed in trouble. Ironically, when I did a burglary with one of the guys we did not trust each other. Although we started out with nothing and then scored for $2,000, we'd want to split everything down to the exact penny and dared someone to stash an extra coin.

I went to Spofford (a juvenile retention center), and from there I later went to Rikers Island C-74 for adolescents. There I learned some of what we called "52", which was a type of boxing style with weird blocks and punches. I never learned it all, though. I learned how to play the wall on a chump.

This place became like a rite of passage for me. I later learned the intimidation game that would later cost me seven years of my life behind bars. An example of the intimidation game was when some new jack came into the jail block and somebody would look at his footwear and step to the new guy saying, "Yo, money. What size are those sneakers?" If the guy showed fear we would tell him, "Yo, you want to fight for them?" It was either a yes or a no. If yes, we'd tell him to play the back and the one with the best knuckle game took all. If he said no, he would be told to "run those kicks." He would then be given a pair of ragged $1.45 pair of shower slippers, or something like them.

One other intimidation game was from behind the gate (cell bars). We called those guys "cell gangsters" until somebody proved them different. One time, this white boy came in real late at night after everybody was locked down. I spotted him first because they assigned him a cell right across from mine. I decided to try the intimidation game. "Yo, money!" I yelled in a real deep voice. The white boy came to the gate. I was wearing a stocking cap and a doo rag on my head that made you look tough then. "Where you from?" I asked him. He appeared scared as he hesitated to answer. "What size are those sneakers?" I asked him. He wore my size (not that it made a difference because this was just a tactic). "7½," he responded real timid. "Yo, run those sneakers or I'm ah bust your f----g s--t on the lock out!" I kept up with the basic cell gate lines. "I'm gonna bust your f----g eye and break your f----g jaw." I screamed a little louder now. "That's word to my mamma! You think I'm bullsh--ting? Kick those sneakers out before I f--k you up." The sneakers came flying out the cell. Wow! This s--t worked. I had the white boy's sneakers.

A few hours later, a suicide watch came by and we saw the white boy crying with a sheet around his neck and tied around something on the ceiling of his cell. He was standing on the sink so he could reach the ceiling. Obviously he was going to attempt to commit suicide. The suicide watch called the police and the white boy was cut down, ridiculed, and moved to an observation unit. This is a perfect example of how stress can make a person react irrationally where at other times it could cause a person to bring out their best.

The other guys laughed at this whole ordeal. They said things like, "That stupid-ass cracker was trying to hang himself", or "Yo, Shaky, you got that nigger before me." I was definitely going to "vic" him (i.e., make him a victim). Part of our rites of passage in prison was to be hard-hearted and rough. It has just stepped up a pace where they stab and rip you with razors quicker. This is almost like a rite of passage for drive-by shooters. We set the trends a long time ago and wonder why the kids are doing what they're doing. They are just a little more ruthless and they will kill a grandmother just as fast as they would a teenager. It's unfortunate, but we have no one to blame but ourselves. When I say ourselves I speak also of the society from which I came from: America.

I was eventually sent to a foster home because the woman my mother left as a guardian could not manage me. I don't like the fact that they sent me to stay with a white family, but I was O.K. for a second.

Later on I was sent to stay with a lady named Gloria. She stayed with a man named Pete who was about 6'8", big, black and weighed about 200 pounds. Gloria was slim, had dark skin, and short hair. She was very nice. She worked with my mother a lot, both in the bars and in the cocaine game. Some of the bars were: Jimmy Daniels on 116th St., Club 18 on 118th St. and Lenox, and a few others. There were grenades and s--t like that at Gloria's house that were probably Pete's. When I saw them I said to myself, "Wow! I wonder what the f--k I could do with this s--t." One thing though, Pete never talked that much. Gloria did all she could to help me and I didn't give her many problems there. I guess there were times that I just wanted to have the best like everybody else. Gloria and Pete were hustlers and they kept the basic necessities like food, plenty of soda and snacks, plus they gave me a few dollars. So, I was content a little. Of course, there was something more that a person like me wanted. I wanted to have more than just the bare necessities. I wanted to have it all.

My mother's time was getting short and she pleaded with the system to give her a furlough to come and check on her oldest boy. I remember how she was when she came to see me. I know one thing: it was a moment that I will never forget. To have some child's mother or father come home from prison on a furlough are the warmest and most fulfilling feeling you can give a child who yearns for that parent.

While my mother was in prison she met a man named Henry Williams who was in prison for shooting a Federal agent five times. Henry was from St. Louis and he was a practicing Moorish American (he had been one of the thirteen Bald Head Moors). They were able to get together in a co-ed facility, and they eventually fell in love and married each other. My mother would give him a son named Justice Williams El.

Finally, my mother came home along with Henry and a baby on the way. We moved to the Bronx on 173rd Street and Macombs Road, Building 15-15 (McClines residence). We never recovered what we lost as a family because of my mother's incarceration. My mother finished her time on parole and we moved to Baltimore, Maryland on Reisterstown Road.

While in Baltimore, I was like a celebrity. I had a different accent when I spoke. I had bought a lot of nice clothing while I was stealing and selling drugs so I had a lot going for myself as a kid entering into a new community. My clothes were not sold in stores because I had most of my pants tailor-made. My friends and I made this a fad. In fact, the styles that we wore eventually became the Oriental and Delancey Street man's specialties. This is something that I saw happen. So when I hear it said that they steal everything that we get or do, I know that it is true; it goes from rap music to dance to styles to culture.

M.S.T. of A.
National Headquarters

I went to school in Baltimore (Frederick Douglas and North Western High). Unfortunately, I didn't finish because my mother became homesick and we moved back to New York. I learned a little about the Moorish Americans while in Baltimore. My mother had met and married a Moor while they were doing federal time.

Baltimore was different than New York City. I could beat anybody with the Three-Card Molly game and I often did. It is a little sad because it's a sucker's game and some of the nicest people can be suckered, whereas under other circumstances you would not take them like that.

While in Baltimore I hooked up with a guy named Roger, who was a burglar. We did a burglary one time and we got a few things, namely some jewelry. What used to get me was that Roger used to like to sit in the victim's homes and watch television, and he would go into their refrigerators looking for food and beverages. Now that I reflect back, I wonder if he was just hungry because there was no food at his home. I never went to Roger's house, although he came to my parents' house all the time. Roger would make sandwiches and cook bacon and eggs. This was strange to me because I was anxious to get out of there but Roger seemed at home. I gave my mother a ring with a diamond in it. I later would have the other jewelry melted down and a medallion and ring set made called Shaky Shake. The medallion and the ring had the name Shake on them. Both had diamond chips in them.

Double Green

When I got back to New York I was a little out of touch. I didn't have the nice clothes and I didn't know what was really going on that much. What I did have was a reputation and all those who were my friends were in tune and on top of the happenings because, just like before, we were the ones who made things happen when nothing was happening. The gang days were no longer it. Neither was the spinning on our heads, as we were getting too big for this now. Toy came to the rescue.

At that time a drug called "Double Green" was popular, so we went and purchased some baking soda, green tape and glycine bags. We made four dummy quarter bags of dope and placed two green strips of tape on the bags. It was about 7 o'clock in the evening on a cold winter night. We went out on 127th St. and Eighth Avenue and began yelling, "Double Green! Double Green!" We sold those four bags in about five seconds at the going rate of $55 a piece. The purchaser wanted a discount of about one dollar, but Toy said, "No!" I looked at him like he was crazy. The man was getting ready to give us $219 dollars for four bags of baking soda. However, just like Toy predicted, the guy figured this must be the real thing. "Alright," he said, "here", and he gave us $220. I admit I felt remorse for what I did. However, it seemed almost like the law of the asphalt jungle that I grew up in. Dope money was still fast money. You had to be ruthless and cold-blooded sometimes in the drug world (also known as the underground world).

Toy and I were out of there. We went and bought two new bomber jackets at A.J. Lesters, and then we went to the Foster Projects to see some chicks named Rhonda, Debbie, Brenda Fee Fee, and Nee Nee. These were some girls we'd grown up with. The best time to see girls was when we were fresh-dipped and had get-high money. This was the in thing for most of us. It was almost like a rite of passage that you had to get high, especially off of reefer; everyone seemed to be doing it. It was even smoked in the open on the street.

We threw parties so we could make some money, but we would never forget our old tricks if things got rough. When we went to the parties we just chilled on the wall and sniffed a little coke at a table somewhere and gave the look as if there would be trouble if anyone approached our table. Dope kids and stickup kids were considered dangerous; they carried tools and it was assumed that they would use them. Washington D.C.'s murder rate validates this.

I stole a little so that I could maintain and get on my feet. I began to smoke angel dust again and by then I had learned a little bit more about the system from the institution. I had run into the juvenile system, I had been in a foster home and in and out of the precinct. This same system had made my mother do time. The messages of the sixties' radicals still rang clear in my ears and underneath all the drugs I still heard, "Pigs! Devils!" Three of the worst moments in my life were: 1) when my mother was stripped of her freedom, her pride was shattered and dignity punctured by a cracker judge, and she was sent away. I sat there, watched, and cried, 2) when a cracker judge did the same thing to me and my mother was forced to sit and watch. She and I cried on both occasions. I imagine my ancestors went through this same type of s--t in the motherland and upon reaching this land and 3) when the court came back with a guilty verdict for something I didn't do and sentenced me with the words: "The system is not perfect, but it's the only system we've got."

My mother was not selling drugs anymore. She still did not have a diploma, as far as I know, and she was receiving welfare or working on a job that paid little or nothing. Things were rough. I could not see myself as a big boy or a young man who was old enough to help bring about change and do nothing. I decided that the least I could do was drop out of school and do for myself. Besides, what were they teaching me in school anyway? Nothing really!

The Straw That
Broke the Camel's Back

The straw that broke the camel's back was when they had black history week at Benjamin Franklin High School. I had learned about the Moorish American philosophy which stated that we should not be called black, Negro, Ethiopian or colored because these were names placed upon us during the time of slavery and they were not names of any race or nationality. I was taught that when a German comes over to America he is called a German-American, or a French person a French-American, etc. I spoke with the principal about this and he appeared to be what was then considered a token Negro, house nigger, or a brainwashed individual. He disagreed with me and thought I was crazy. I believe he held it against me. He wanted me to be left back a grade after I had already completed two thirds of the semester. I told him that I heard of being skipped or being left back, but I had never heard of someone being in the 11th grade doing 2/3 of the semester and then going back to the 10th grade, so I left school. I tried to enter Taft High School and other schools but I just didn't seem to have it for school anymore.

I had more time for the streets after leaving school. I had to survive off of the streets because, although I ate at my mother's, I felt it was my responsibility to do for myself. In addition, my mother was not able to provide me with the many things that I wanted. She wasn't selling drugs anymore, so it was hard. My mother has never had anyone to really help her. She struggled with her kids solo!

The community that I grew up in said that you had to have it like the Feds (i.e., be wealthy). I moved out of my mother's apartment when one day she and I got into an argument. It was more or less one of those times when a mother says, "I pay the rent here and you are going to do as I say do." My response was the typical, "Listen, I am getting older now. I am a man." It was much more than that, though. Pressure bursts pipes and this system is designed to pressure and bust up the black family. I left and got a lease from someone I knew; this was all that the welfare department wanted. I paid the landlord a little here and a little there for looking out for me. I opened up a spot called the "Slot Spot." This was a source of income for me and started me on my way to the rebirth of the dope game.

The Dope Game

The Slot Spot was a place where I sold angel dust and reefer. I made up a lot of flyers and gave them out all over the neighborhood and at the disco. I gave them out as if it were a legal product that I was selling and I had license to do so. I am sure the police knew about this spot. Most of my regular customers were junior high school students (JHS 82 was across the street). Thank God those kids mostly bought reefer. I had watched young kids shooting heroin and older ones shooting drugs in their necks and groin area because they had a hard time finding a vein. I had watched guys like Jeff, his little brother Manny and his cousin Terry getting drug money, so I wanted some too.

Later on, DeeBo got a lot of Chunky Black and hit me off. Chunky Black was quality reefer. It made your saliva dry, white and sticky like paste. Your spit became caked and it was hard to spit anything out of your mouth. One thing is for sure: you knew you were high, although I don't know why we called taking something that was actually making us depressed "getting high." This reefer made you get the munchies. There were not as many chemicals in the reefer then; as sad as it sounds, I think I would rather just have had the reefer than the newer drugs like crack. Chunky Black was mostly purchasable in Harlem. Therefore, I was in possession of the two drugs that were mostly sold in Harlem, yet also in popular demand where I was in the Bronx.

The Slot Spot drew a lot of customers because of the quality of the Chunky Black and the inaccessibility of the drug in the area. My spot was becoming like 123rd St. between Lenox and 7th Avenue: cars began pulling up in the middle of the night. I bought some DJ equipment and constantly pumped music to lure customers in. There was a hole placed in the door where the customer could put their money and then they would get their product. All day I would say, "Put your money in the hole."

The problem was that the police were watching and were able to take pictures; I decided to do something about this. I went to the lumberyard and the hardware store and ordered some large two-by-fours, a bunch of long nails, some wood, and some bells and buzzers, and I built another door with a walkway about the size of a prison cell, which is about a 12' x 8' area.

Afterwards, if customers wanted something they would ring the bell and I would buzz them inside this hole. They would step inside and they would be stuck in this little 12' x 8' area. "Close the door," I would tell them. Then I would ask them, "How many do you want?" They would tell me what they wanted and stick their money through the hole of the second door that was not visible to the police. The customers would get their product, be buzzed out, and then leave.

The Slot Spot was an example of the ingenuity of a young black boy surviving in the city of New York. I was only fifteen and four other people older than me had been unsuccessful with this spot. It was becoming a success for me. I often wonder how much money went through my hands then. The problem was I became lax and fell victim to using my own supply. At this time I was smoking about fifteen bags of angel dust a day. When I went to visit my mother she noticed that I had lost a lot of weight. My mother contacted my stepfather and he came up to the Bronx to get me before I shriveled up and withered away. I look back now and thank God that I had someone there who cared. I had seen others who were in the same situation that I was in and they unfortunately did not have the help from someone who cared. Many brothers and sister died because nobody came to their aid when they needed them most.

Youth Council President

After a period of recuperation, I got involved with a youth council organization in the Metro North Riverview Projects. I always liked to be outspoken so it was not hard for me to land the spot of president of the youth council. My opponent received the vice president position and my brother received the treasurer position. We asked the manager of the complex if he would allow us to throw a fundraiser. He said that the only available days were: one in the week coming up and others months away. I asked him if he would allow us to have the day that was coming up that week. He expressed to me that it would not be enough time to plan and organize for the party. *Ha! Ha!* I laughed to myself. Then, in a polite manner I asked, "Well, could you just give us the date anyway? There is nothing to lose, right?" So he gave it to us, it seemed out of spite, in hopes that we wouldn't accomplish anything.

My brothers, friends and associates gave out flyers all over the place, so almost every building within a 25-block radius had a flyer in it. The party was packed and there was not enough room to hold everyone. I was a natural when it came to organizing and campaigning, but I could not have succeeded without the help of others. The word on the east side and the west side was: "Yo. Shaky and them are giving a party." My brother and a few friends kept security and there were no problems that night. After that day, though, there were problems with the youth council organization. I honestly believe that the tenants became afraid of us doing what they should have been doing all along for the youth in the community. I was told that I was too old to work with the youth council, as I had just turned 18. Ironically, the manager placed someone who was 35 years old to be in charge.

Shortly after that I developed another youth council organization, but all we had was a clubhouse for our meetings; we were using a shack that someone had built out of wood. I became discouraged and began getting involved with negative things again.

Then I went to the Bronx and organized a youth organization in my apartment. Every Sunday I would go to the kids' apartments and I would ask their parents if they could come to my apartment for the day. The parents liked this idea and before I knew it I had a house full of kids. I used to buy apples, milk, pizza, candy, etc for them, and the kids would dunk their heads for apples. God blessed us with a piano: while snooping around in an abandoned building that had caught fire (looking for copper pipes and marble stairs to sell), I found one that was in perfect condition with the exception of a missing piano leg. I paid someone to help me get the piano in my house. Every Sunday we would make up songs and sing them at the piano. One of the songs was entitled, *Keep On Loving and Don't Stop the Loving*. The kids would also read from both the Koran (Moorish American version) and the Bible books with the pictures for children. I was amazed to see some kids who had problems reading in school read exceptionally well when they were with me. I even remember going to tell one of the parents that his child could read very well because I had heard and watched him, when his teacher had said he couldn't read.

The problem was that none of the parents sent the children with any money. I could not afford to support the program I had started. I began to think of ways to keep it up. I even spoke with the landlord, Elouise, about helping me to get a pony for the kids. I tried to justify the way I felt: why should only white people have these types of things (ponies and horses)? She agreed to keep the pony in the backyard. I went around begging for quarters.

I figured that if I could just get someone to help me, I could do something constructive in the community. I organized some brothers that I knew and we all went to Congressman Charles Rangle to speak with him about an abandoned building we were willing to fix up for a large youth organization. He didn't give us a positive response and all I know is that we left there feeling mighty low. I decided that maybe I could rob a supermarket and use the money from that to build another youth council organization. I thought that if I got the money I could buy a community room or something like that. At the time I was using drugs a little. I don't know which motivated me the most: the desire to build the youth organization or the drugs. Well, I was through begging all of these grown folks for anything and I made up my mind: I would rob a grocery store and use the money to do something positive (buy a church). I borrowed a toy gun from G.G. (one of the kids who used to come to my house).

I went into the grocery store and announced a stickup. I had a girl with me and everything went smooth, or at least I thought so. I had never been taught to back out of the store after getting the money. I moved so fast that I didn't notice that people came out behind me and got a make on the license plate. We were caught about twenty blocks away. When the policeman asked me what the hell was going on during the investigative interview I told him that I was trying to get money for a church. He and his co-workers began laughing. I tried to tell them what I was feeling and trying to do, but they really didn't care. I was just some bugged-out nigger kid to them. That was my first felony.

The Breaking of a Man

That was the second time that my mother and I cried. I was arraigned in court and my mother was there. I sat on a bench with a crown on my head, a gift my mother had made for me. It was black with space-like designs on it. It had diagrams symbolic of a half moon, stars and planets, or other stellar matter. I had embellished it a little by taking costume jewelry and putting it into the crown. The jewelry looked like different colored precious gems. All in all, the crown looked like the one that the Honorable Elijah Muhammad used to wear.

I thought I was going home, but I was remanded. At that moment I felt a part of me stripped away. I snatched the crown off of my head in anger, threw it away and began crying. Actually, the crown meant a lot to me. My mother had made it in Baltimore and it had sentimental value. However, I was now mad and thinking very irrationally. My mother began crying because she couldn't post the bail that was set, which I believe was $300. When I went back to the bullpens I told the court officer to place me in the homosexual pins. I was traumatized, crushed, and my spirit was broken. I felt like less than a man to have a cracker tell me in front of my mother that he was sending me back to the f-----g dog cage. I wish I had had a better understanding of Jesus Christ and salvation then. I wish I had known and understood that in *him* I have a crown that no judge or man can take away, because he is the King of Kings and I am his royal child, bought with his blood.

Little did I know what I was about to embark upon. I do not wish the feelings I had on anyone, or the things I was about to go through. I was about to enter into another dimension of evil and demonic spirits. I must confess that it was not all good. These people had power and it had nothing to do with that sign that said, "In God we trust." We truly are fighting spiritual wickedness in high places and it is only through divine power that we can win.

Homo

I could not think of a politically correct term to name this chapter. Might as well call it like it is, a spade is a spade by any other name. Furthermore, a spade will remain a spade, but with Jesus Christ one can be changed. To those of you reading this book that feel you cannot change: the devil is a liar and there is no truth in him. It is a trick of the enemy to keep you in bondage.

I began to exhibit the behavior of a person that really didn't care. I never really figured out exactly why I got into homosexuality. There appeared to be either a little freak in me, a hell of a lot of confusion, or it was just a matter of curiosity. I wasn't sure where a man should draw the line as it pertained to showing love for his brothers. To what extent should one go? It seemed that this question was more at the forefront than the question of who I was or what was my true identity. Was I looking for love in the wrong places? Was I just curious and searching? Was I projecting all the hurt that I felt subconsciously? The devil had me bound and was playing tricks with my mind. If there is anyone out there confused and has the same questions, let me save you the journey. If you feel you have to get into an intimate sexual relationship with a partner of the same sex to show your love for that person, then you are too far over to the left. You need to draw a big line right there and pray that God will deliver you and bind up that trickster devil, for he is a sly old fox. If I had my way I'd put him in a box, lock the door and throw away the key for all the tricks he's played on me. I'm glad I am converted and trusting in the Lord.

First of all, I must confess that it's truly painful to tell this story. The stigma attached to this whole subject of homosexuality amongst black men is devastating, to say the least. I have never met anyone who said, "I understand."

I was confused as to whether or not it was permissible to show love to one's brothers by way of sexual gratification. This led to a quick phase of experimenting with more than just the question. I believe that psychologists knew what they were talking about when they spoke about one's environment having an effect on an individual, especially when a person is still young and searching for certain basic answers in life. Hence, my being in that environment (i.e., homo unit) pretty much set the stage for the outcome. To give you a basic description, the place was a regular jail set up with cells that contained a cot to sleep on, a sink, and a toilet. There were approximately 30 men to each unit. There were some men who were dressed just like women: they had enlarged their chests to look like women's breasts, some of their faces appeared to be as smooth as a woman's, and their voices were octaves higher than a guy's voice. The officers there not only allowed the men to have lipstick, eyeliner and other makeup accessories, but the officers also brought some in for the inmates. Then there were those guys that signed up in there because they did not consider themselves homosexuals because they did not receive, but rather pitched. I told you the devil is a sly fox. When inmates were locked out for recreation they were placed in a dormitory setting. It is hard to believe that right there in the dorm, in the open area, the inmates were having sexual encounters. The cells remained open and, to my surprise, the officers would be in the cells having sex with inmates. Talk about a corrupt system! Is this what we call rehabilitation or corrections? Thanks, but no thanks.

Some may say that I'm in denial; however, I do not feel I actually set myself up for this. I didn't really make a conscious decision to go there. Although I wasn't coerced to go, I maintain that there were circumstances that led up to my making that irrational decision. Had the circumstances been different I don't think that I would have been in that predicament.

There I was in C-74 (homo unit) trying to figure things out. I automatically found myself fighting with guys I didn't know, and I still don't remember to this day what the fights were about. My first fight was with a Spanish bully. He was a little taller than I was and we were in a big cage along with some other guys. We were about to eat. As soon as it was time to set it off, I immediately tore into the kid. My blood was boiling and I was full of anxiety. I jumped on him like an animal and he tried to duck my attack. I then bit him as hard as I could on his back and held my teeth clenched there. The fight was over a few minutes later because I wouldn't let go of my pit bull lock.

Contestant number two was a guy who was my size. We were both squared off in a little area. The guy was riffing with me about something that I cannot recall. I was just standing there with my hands in my pockets. Then Rob-o called over to me and said, "Yo! Take your hands out of your pockets if you're going to fight." I was on front street because a lot of people could see us from the windows and bars and the little area that separated the two dorms. So I took my hands out of my pockets while feeling the peer pressure. I didn't really want to fight. I never liked real fighting (I loved slap boxing and boxing in the ring). I was faster and smarter than many in any game of outwitting your opponent. Real fighting made me think of murder, which is why I think I feared it most.

So once I took my hands out of my pockets, I noticed my opponent positioning himself to attack. Right then, at that precise moment, my instincts kicked in and the adrenaline started flowing through me. I responded quick and explosive. I lifted my left leg (as the right-handed pitcher does in baseball just before throwing a fast ball) and brought my right African soup bone from way back in the Congo. I let loose an overhand right which connected full flesh with his eye. He went down low to my legs, trying to recover. I immediately took him down to the ground and held him still. We were clinched together on the ground, eye to eye. I told him, "I'll bite your f----g eye out!" As I said this, I almost licked my K-9 tooth on the right side of my jaw. We stayed there for a minute, and I let him up. The fight was over. His face was hurt. However, I did not feel a sense of victory, really, but rather a sense of compassion.

By then the environment was beginning to have an influence on me at a deeper subconscious level. I didn't pay a lot of things attention that I used to before I settled in. Many things were routine and I really had begun to function in that environment as if there were nothing wrong. This was when I asked myself the question: *should man love his brother to the extent that he should sexually gratify him, out of that deep desire and love for brotherhood?* Talk about ethical dilemmas!

This may seem like a stupid question to some or an easy one to others. However, being young in a homosexual environment such as the one that I was in, where homosexual acts where taking place all day everyday in the open, made things confusing for me. I was left vulnerable, coming from a background such as mine, never having discussed this subject with another older male figure. In this battle, I somehow came to the conclusion that I would try it and see.

To many I should not feel guilty in having said yes to my question. And, in fact, they may see it as a unique and special quality in that I would go as far as to give myself for peace and brotherhood. However, some will think of me as being less than a man, stupid, and abnormal. I just wanted to be loved and to show love to all people. It saddens me to think that many good people will probably totally disassociate themselves from me and prejudge me based on this experience. In fact, I will probably never have friendships that I could have had otherwise, if I did not speak the truth. However, if it will help save someone else then it's okay with me. This is a hurting feeling and I can imagine what those who are gay go through everyday of their lives with constant discrimination and disrespect. I am not saying this to condone homosexuality, because I do not; however, I do not think that we ought to be judge and jury and be homophobic. My hope is that in reading this book some homosexuals will do a self-assessment, repent and be born again. If they do, I hope that they won't let anybody turn them around.

The next day I saw the guy I had hit in the eye; he had a very big shiner. After I did what I thought was critical thinking I walked over to him and propositioned him. I was a little nervous, but I got it out. I don't remember what I said exactly, only that the word love was mentioned, which is what I felt I was about to give. In my mind I was about to perform (I felt at that time) love for my brother.

I don't want to use drugs as an excuse either, but I wonder how much my overall use of drugs up to that point might have affected my ability to reason.

Naturally, due to the environment, he accepted my proposition, and this was the first time I found myself on the other end of homosexuality. I performed orally in front of others for this was the norm of that subculture within the prison society.

Afterwards, I was shown a big lead pipe that this same individual had gotten and had planned on splitting my wig with later on that day. It was as if I had crossed over into another world, and it would take some time before I found my way back home. Talk about the prodigal son: I did more than sleep with pigs; I was sleeping with the enemy.

In some cases there is just no crossing back over once you've crossed over. The reality is that there are probably more brothers than we know who have crossed over and back, but very few would let such a thing be known. To have crossed back over is to realize that this is not now and never was right in the first place. However, you feel a sense of guilt and shame for having ever made that journey, and you want to be accepted by others for who you are despite your mistakes and shortcomings. Unfortunately, people want you to be perfect before they can accept you. You have to be down and fit with the crowd. The same way there were many brothers who wanted to cross back over that ocean and go back to Africa but they could not swim the 9,000 miles, is the same way we have lost a lot of good brothers who have crossed over to the homosexual lifestyle and find it too hard to get back. To them I say: come to your senses and ask God to deliver you. I am a living witness that he can do it.

This event marked the beginning of people viewing me differently. I was now considered a punk, a faggot, and not a man. For example, I was once caught off guard in the homo-quad. This big, scary, pitbull-looking motherf---r hauled off and slapped the piss s--t out of me. He then demanded that I perform oral sex on him. Now, I had heard of "fight or get in flight," but in this scenario a third option came into my mind: perform. Actually, fighting didn't appear to come to my mind. I was shocked and frozen. I knew that flight was not an option because where was I going to run to in a prison, where the police were down with the program and were having sex with the young brothers? Unfortunately, I was thrown completely out of focus. I was afraid and confused, so I performed. Eventually I fought this same individual one-on-one and, to my surprise, I handled him well and he didn't bother me anymore.

I had very little experience in this area (i.e., homosexuality) on the giving end; I was somewhat confused for about eight months and in search of my identity. I was lost. I guess this is why I like the song that says, "I once was lost, but now I am found."

Eventually, I was released and because of the confined environment many people did not know what I had gone through. However, I did speak with my family about this experience and, to my surprise, they did not bash me or ridicule me, but rather they showed compassion and tried to understand. A guy named Heavy and his mother also spoke with me.

Somehow, finally I snapped out of that trance. It is strange how many men have done what was done to me to women. In fact, I am sure there are many women who can empathize with the feeling of having this happen to them (i.e., being violated). I *do* think that the ramifications are socially and politically worse when it happens to a man. With a woman one may feel as though it is justified (maybe) by some natural male animal instinct in his attraction to the opposite sex. However, with men it is sick. For little children to desire or think it is cool to do these things is something that we need to take a closer look at in this society. Whether it goes back to a collective unconscious or some socio-cultural thing, it needs to be addressed. I am sure some brothers and sisters never return from their journey through the unknown.

I am very grateful to my family for their efforts in attempting to understand me while I was in such a confused state of mind. They were so supportive and may God reward each of them for that. My friends, too, did not disown me; they figured it was just the angel dust. I don't know if it was the prison, the courts, the drugs, other things, a combination of them all, or just fate. Maybe it was just one of those things where we say, "What goes around comes around." I am glad that it is over.

Nevertheless, I have learned a hell of a lot in prison and much of this came from personal experience. I learned of some things, while in there, that can make a man and some that can break a man. I would return to prison several more times and each time it would be different.

While in jail I learned how to be slicker and more knowledgeable of the criminal life. I received interned supervision, which is a form of probation. This did not last very long: I lost focus of the old goals and basically I was just concerned about self and survival. I continued to get high and steal little things to make it from time to time. I did little odd jobs and received public assistance (I felt the government owed it to me).

Victoria

I met Victoria in Benjamin Franklin High School around my first year there. What I remember most about Victoria is that she had what we called a "chicken breast" (her boobs were very big). I liked big-breasted girls. She also had a pretty smile with shining white teeth. I remember trying to talk to her once but I wasn't really on her because I was in popular demand among the girls; this may have been because I had angel dust then. Although I was in popular demand, I wasn't getting any sex nor had I gotten much of any. One day Victoria approached me after school and practically seduced me. She asked me to come with her to her house. She lived in a nice co-op in the Bronx called The Village, on the first floor. She had a terrace, and the building had guards that said, "Hello, Ms. Doomis" when she came in. This was new for me, but I just went along with everything like it wasn't no thang.

Victoria's mother was at work and I guess Victoria just "had to have it," as Spike Lee said. I think that that was my third piece of trim. Victoria had a strong odor that acted as an aphrodisiac and she loved to ride, which was okay with me.

Victoria and I started seeing each other mainly there at her mother's house. I don't recall ever asking Victoria to be my woman, but who needed formalities? Basically she was my girl because we were swinging episodes together. One day I met her father when he stopped in early from work. I was well mannered, so I simply said, "Good evening, sir." He spoke and kept stepping as if to say: *you're f----g my daughter, right? That is enough, you don't have to f--k or stroke me too.*

Victoria and I parted the same way we got together. It was informal; we just stopped seeing each other. I guess it may have been my jealousy because I always thought that the girls were going to be sexing someone else.

After getting Victoria out of my system, I thought it was over. All of a sudden, one day out of the clear blue sky, one of my brothers called me: "Grayling some girl is at the door to see you." When I went to the door and saw Victoria I was surprised. For one thing, I didn't even know she knew where my mother lived. Victoria explained to me that her mother had thrown her out of the house and she needed somewhere to stay. I told her I'd talk to my mother. So I went to my mother and I said, "Mommy, my girlfriend was thrown out and she has nowhere to stay. Do you mind if she stayed here with us for a while?" Surprisingly, my mother agreed to my request. I calculated having p---y on a regular basis for the first time since we would be literally sleeping together every night. I figured that was the least Victoria could do for me.

Once again Victoria was my girl, unofficially and without my requesting her to be. I bought her everything I could while she stayed there. I washed the dirty dishes we ate out of, and I washed the clothes. Victoria was living like a queen for a while. However, one day I came in and I asked Victoria to fix me something to eat because I was hungry. I remember it was some fried chicken that I wanted. She refused, so I asked my sister, but my mother was listening to the conversation (she had been clocking our interactions ever since the time she allowed Victoria to stay in her home). My mother didn't like what she heard. "Grayling!" my mother called me to her side. "You can stay here but that girl can't stay here no more." "Okay," I said to my mother.

I found a place for Victoria and me to stay in the Bronx: 15-15 Macombs Road. We stayed together for about 2 1/2 years. We got high together off of rum and coke, pina colada, reefer, cocaine, and angel dust. We had some good times together, but some times became very trying for us, especially when we were smoking angel dust because we didn't know if we were coming or going with that s--t. We would argue about things that did not make any sense or argue for nothing and swear that there were actually some grounds for an argument.

I remember one time Victoria must have been very afraid of me because angel dust can give you distorted facial features and distort your perception of reality. Whatever the case was, I assume that she was afraid because she had gotten a pair of scissors to defend herself against me. When I saw the scissors I only remembered the law of the land: do not allow anyone to pull anything on you without using it yourself. So I immediately had an adrenaline rush, and I rushed her. I took the scissors and stabbed her. I had never done this before to anyone. I felt very bad after I did it. The only reason I remember doing it was because I felt that this was the thing to do when someone pulled out a weapon on you. This was a learned behavior and response more so than anything else. I don't know or remember the actual reason why she was afraid. It could have been that she was just dusted up and paranoid, which is another one of the effects of the drug. We used to smoke the dust on top of smoking reefer, drinking, and sometimes sniffing coke. The more "get high", the better. When you are a get-high person infected with this disease that this society has entrapped many in with its wicked web of crime, corruption, racism, and systematic genocide, you never have much of a chance. We were born inside the barricades of the ghetto. Many of the generations before us never made it out of that hellhole that they had not chosen.

There were many other incidents between Victoria and I, but there is another in particular that stands out. She wanted to go out with her friends and asked me, I guess out of respect since I was paying the bills at the time. I guess she respected me as the man, even if my sense of manhood was distorted. "OK," I told her. "But just don't come in here all pissy-drunk at any time of the morning." Well, I'll be dammed if it wasn't like a self-fulfilling prophecy coming right before my eyes. The next morning Victoria came home at 6:00 a.m. in a cab outside beeping its horn. When I went outside to pay for the cab Victoria emerged, barely able to stand up. She was pissy-drunk and talking in riddles. I was embarrassed and fuming because although we got high we tried to be mature about it and not be spaced-out in the street; we tried to maintain some sort of pride and dignity despite our addiction. So I took Victoria upstairs and as we got in the house I was already bitching as loud as I could. "What the f--k is this s--t, Victoria?" She slurred, all drunk, "Did you pay the cab?" I tried to talk reasonably and use logic in an illogical situation. I continued to speak with her, "Victoria, didn't I ask you not to do this? Where were you?" "Pelham Bay Hotel," she said. "What! What the f--k were you doing in a hotel? With who? I thought you told me that you were going somewhere with your girlfriends." She told me an incoherent story about some guys wanting to take her and her friends to this hotel. She said that she tried to get out of the car but she couldn't. She told me that she was able to get out of the hotel because she was asked to go and get some ice. She said she had not done anything. I went for this until I had sex with her and her p---y was like an ocean. I had no idea that this may have been a normal thing that happens with women. As far as I was concerned, she'd been f----g and I told her as much. I told her I was going to bust her a-- in the morning. In the morning I started some s--t with Victoria about her being at some hotel with some niggers. She became very sassy in her hangover, and I didn't take kindly to this attitude. One thing led to another and I ended up hitting her with the back of one of my Pierre Cardin shoes. The bottom of the shoe had a very heavy sole and the sole pierced her skin. She had to get stitches for this mark. Once again I felt sorry for what I had done, but what good would it do?

Not too long after this, Victoria became pregnant and I was confused about whether or not the child she was carrying was mine.
I asked her whose child it was and she said it was my child. Later, as it neared the time of delivery, I asked her again, "Victoria, tell me something. Whose baby is it?" She responded very angrily, "It's my f----g baby, that's whose. No, it ain't yours, it's mine." I was thinking in the back of my mind, "It's probably someone else's. I probably can't make any babies. It's probably one of those guys who she was in the hotel with." I started counting back the months to the time she had gone out and stayed at the hotel. I did all of this in a matter of a second after her

answer. I punched her in the middle of her forehead when she told me that s--t. I said, "What the f--k do you mean it ain't mine when you are sleeping here every f----g night?" This all happened simultaneously: the thinking, punching, and talking. Then I left the house to get away before I did something that I might have regretted.

I returned to find the piano torn apart. Every key was broken. I called out, "Victoria! Victoria!" but she didn't answer. So I began to look around because I felt she was still there. I found her in a closet hiding like a little kid; she had this big knot right in the center of her little forehead. She looked like a three-eyed cyclops. It looked so sad and ridiculous that all I could do was laugh at her, even though I was VERY UPSET. I was mainly upset because I played the piano with the kids and played it whenever I was stressed and could not blame Victoria or find anyone else to blame for the frustration I was feeling. I was angry because I felt that I should have been somewhere else in life; that I was not cut out for this type of life; that I was naturally a kind and loving person who could not seem to find kindness and love amongst the forest of mass confusion.

Eventually, despite our hazy maze, we worked things out and Victoria gave birth to our daughter Crystal (Too Tough) Doomis (Ferrand) on Friday February 13, 1982 in Lincoln Hospital. Things went all right for a few months until my birthday.

Happy Birthday

It was the dream of every ghetto kid that sold drugs at one time or another to survive to that day when they would strike it Robert; the day that the struggle and suffering would end with the big money rolling in. I would then have the cars and everything that Hollywood showed, just like the Robert and the famous had. No more poverty and misery. But it was all a dream, like the many dreams that our ancestors had but never saw become reality. Though they all try to achieve their dreams through obstacles and by any possible means, 99.99% of the ghetto children never succeed.

I worked a day or two, part time, cleaning the hallways of my building to get some money. Sometimes I would clean but not get paid. Every time I tried to hustle and make that big mark, things just didn't seem to work out and the dream was usually shattered by some immediate displeasure. If things got bad I could always soup some tokens or go hit some supermarkets. I spoke with Victoria about hustling; I told her that it would probably be best to sell the baby's milk that we received from the WIC program and use the money to buy drugs. Victoria agreed with me to try this little plan as she realized that we didn't have much. I guess Victoria had every right to be upset with me because I helped destroy her life. She believed in me when she bore my child. She believed in me when she agreed to sell the baby milk to add that money to the money needed to re-up our drug supply. It wasn't much of a re-up, because how much could you buy with some money from one child's supply of baby milk at a discount price? Not much. It wasn't the amount that counted. Truth is: we just wanted to get high.

On May 18, 1982 (the night of my birthday), I committed another robbery, more out of frustration than anything else. My baby's mother did not want to spend time with me and she seemed to be non-caring. However, it was more than that, but I couldn't see it then. I was drugging with a newborn baby just coming into my life, my first-born at that. I tried to juggle drugs, but I was getting high on my own supply and this caused conflict and made things worse than they otherwise may have been. I just wanted to spend the night with Victoria and the child, but in my mind she wanted to give me her behind to kiss. The truth is that I failed Victoria and myself, but I couldn't see that then. I figured it was just that time of the month, who knows?

That night I went to jail. I wrote constantly and thought of changing. I was bailed out three months later, only to find Victoria in our bed with another man. I put him out and tried to reason with her. It was over.

The next morning while I was resting, she grabbed the baby and left to stay with her mother, so she could continue seeing her lover. I tried to see my daughter, but her mother and grandmother called the police and told them that I had been giving my 3-month-old daughter cocaine, angel dust, and heroin. I tried to argue in my defense, but the male police, who wanted to make themselves look good in front of these women, simply busted me upside the head with their clubs. I left, bleeding and swollen.

I left Victoria, her mother, the baby, and her boyfriend alone. A couple of days later I tried again because I really wanted to try with her. I wanted to settle down at a very young age. I really didn't like the life I was living. I tried to reason with her, but I guess that guy she had was eating her p---y really good. Besides, I didn't give her that type of pleasure often, maybe I should have. Victoria had both of our noses open.

I once waited for her little boyfriend to come out because I felt we should have a talk. The guy, knowing that I was outside waiting for him, tried to sneak out the back. That day I had on a pinstriped black jacket with padded shoulders. I was wearing some nice pants and a pair of black Pierre Cardin leather shoes (the pair that I had hit Victoria with). On the bottom of the shoes, on both the front and back, were silver taps. I was also strapped with my 32-caliber pistol. I ran around to the back and caught him. "Yo! Yo, homeboy! Let me speak with you for a minute. Check this out. My name is Shake. The girl you f----g with is the mother of my kid. I want you to know that I am not a sucker. I don't want to have to blow nothing up over her. The truth is that I love her and my daughter and I would like you to leave her alone." I slightly showed him the print of my pistol as I said this. Victoria looked from her terrace and started throwing eggs because she wanted me to leave her friend alone. He got the message. He stopped coming around and told Victoria that he really didn't want any trouble. Although Victoria was upset about this, she respected it. However, we did not get together.

Starvin' Manny

I ended up hustling for a minute downtown. I got an apartment on 119th St. and St. Nicholas Avenue: a friend of the family's named Mona was leaving the apartment and gave it to me and my brother Stay High (I kept the apartment in the Bronx too). The apartment was fully furnished, with paneling on the wall and carpet on the floor. It was a beauty. My brother and I were working for this cat called Starvin' Manny, who later died in a hail of bullets. Jealousy, I guess. Anyway, we worked on a salary-selling heroin. Things had changed in the dope game. We got paid off of each bag; for example, 20% or two dollars off every $10 bag. Well, we were pumping quarters of dope a hundred miles an hour. We earned about $25 dollars a day for pocket money and got paid $500 dollars at the end of the week.

I had never seen money coming so fast. Starvin' Manny's spot had people lining up to get serviced. We were inside of an abandoned apartment and we had two escape routes. The customers came from all over. Sometimes they would come and ask for as many as 20 quarters of dope at $50 a piece. That is $1,000 dollars, with no shorts. We had to count that money and count it fast because there were lines of customers waiting. If we took too long we risked the chance of the police seeing a line that was too long to go unnoticed (although they noticed anyway). My brother stayed outside sometimes and watched for the police, and at other times I watched for them. We had passwords to let each other know we were coming. For example, I would say "pretty birds" if the police were anywhere around or if they were just passing by at a distance. If the police came too close to the spot I would yell repeatedly and very loudly, "Birds in flight! Birds in flight!" and my brother would grab the money and drugs and be out before the police even came into the building. The whole thing was something else. I once yelled, "Birds in flight!" as the policed approached the building. A policeman just jumped out of the car and punched me right in the face. This was a detective. I didn't say or do anything. I'd rather have taken that punch than to say anything, knowing that my brother was inside of the spot.

I knew from personal knowledge of how the drug game went that my brother and I were not making the actual money we should have been making. So every time someone asked for a rip down, which is a quarter ripped right down the middle, I would take about $3 to $5 worth of dope and place it inside of a plastic cigarette pack. At the end of the day when we got our $25, I left with about half a bag of dope at least. I would stop once I got to about half. To me, this evened the score.

One day I was not at the spot, my brother went to work alone. I was up at the apartment on 119th St. Somebody came to me and said, "Yo, Shake! Your brother Arty was shot. They blew his leg off with a shotgun, close range." I started flipping. I wanted to kill something just at the sound of it. I had never known anyone close to me who was seriously hurt or who died. None of my immediate blood relatives had ever died that I knew of (other than my father, whom I never knew). So, it was strange for me to hear that. I didn't know what it was like to lose an uncle, mother, grandparent, etc.

I found out that my brother was actually hit with a rifle, and he hadn't lost his leg. He was hit in the leg and ended up with a rod in it. Stay High was working the spot when somebody came to stick him up. The guy got the draw on him, but Stay High refused to give him the quarters of dope. So, the guy shot him. When the police arrived, Stay High was unconscious and had a pocket full of dope and money. They tried to charge him, but because he was unconscious he beat the case, with a good lawyer named Money Roberts.

When my brother finally got out of the hospital Starvin' Manny wanted him to pay for the joints (i.e., quarters) that he had gotten arrested with and did not want to pay my brother for that week. I was not having it. In my mind a person who went out like that, if anything, should be given a position as opposed to being treated like that. I went across town and talked with my mother's husband (Henry, at that time) and told him what was up. He agreed that Manny was out of his f----g mind and that Manny needed to forget about the quarters of dope that the police took. Hence, after a little bit of reasonable talk, my brother was paid for the week he worked and the dope the police had confiscated was forgotten about. After this payment, it was chill out time for my brother and me. One thing that amazed me most about that spot was the ability we had to count money so fast while servicing what must have been hundreds of people a day.

Your Daughter Too

Meanwhile, I was going back and forth to my other apartment in the Bronx; in fact, we used to hang out there after working in the Starvin' Manny spot.

A couple of months later, as I was preparing for work, I heard a knock at the door. I was living alone at the time and just cooling. I did not have many people coming to my home, if any. Therefore, I had no idea who this could be knocking at my door. I went to the door and asked, "Who is it?" Lo and behold, the response came back, "Victoria." I was perplexed as I opened the door. I greeted her as if she were neither friend nor foe. "What's up?" I asked her. I noticed that she had our daughter off to the side in a stroller, as if she were hiding her and was going to surprise me. All of a sudden Victoria said, "Here! She is your daughter too. You take care of her too." "What?" I asked her in a startled tone. "How are you going to just come here tonight like this? I have to go to work tonight." I was I working as a janitor at that time. In addition, at various times I received public assistance, I hustled, and I did strip dancing (which was where I had to go that night).

Victoria pulled out two knives that she had taken from my mother's apartment. These knives were in a wooden case and they crossed into the letter X, like a two-edged sword. I looked at Victoria as if she was crazy and she looked at me as if she were as well. I asked, "What are you going to do, stab me?" She did not answer me and looked as if she were desperate, scared, and on the verge of something. I simply said to her, "Leave me the baby." She left, and there I was with Too Tough and the stroller. It was Friday night. I guess Victoria just wanted to do a little bump and grind at some disco with some jock. I believe the Whop or the Smurf was the dance out at that time.

It was this day that I first honestly believed in my heart that this was my little girl (biologically). It was something about the way Victoria had said, "She is your daughter too." From that moment on, that baby and I became like white-on-rice, until a series of extraordinary events took place and ruined any chance of us ever being close again.

Everywhere I went my daughter was there with me. I used an Indian pouch thing that straps onto your body and allows you to carry a child around like a kangaroo does. I kept Too Tough strapped to either my back or chest, close to my heart. More often than not she was strapped to my chest because I loved to look into her pretty little innocent star-like eyes.

We became so close. She was like the friend I had always searched for but could never find *and* she was my daughter. The bonding that took place was beautiful and much more than the type that is explained to you in a child development course. I mean we were literally eye-to-eye when I spoke to her. She rested her little head on my shoulders when she was tired. She wasn't walking yet but I did some stretches with her legs and helped her stand very early on. She was never a problem; she was good with me.

Two months had gone by and I hadn't seen Victoria. Too Tough began looking very ill. Her temperature seemed to be high because her head felt very warm. Her eyes appeared to droop very sadly. I began to panic and get scared. I had learned early on how to change diapers and feed a child because of all my little siblings, but this was something I had never experienced. "What's wrong, baby?" I asked her while looking into her eyes. But she was too young to talk. She was only 5 1/2 months old and only her eyes spoke to me. I received the message, *Get help. My God, what am I going to do?* I asked myself. I had grown to love Too Tough so much, and I knew this then.

I snatched her up and went to a neighbor named Regina, was a registered nurse. She felt Too Tough's head and knew that Too Tough was running a fever. She advised me to take her to the hospital, which I did immediately. I arrived at Bronx Lebanon Hospital with this demanding look and asked for some assistance. I was a young father in love with his daughter who was ill.

I explained that my daughter was sick. They asked me for my daughter's birth certificate; I told them that I did not have it. I explained to them that the mother had come over, pulled out a knife on me and demanded that I take the baby. I told them that I had not seen the mother since then and that she had the birth certificate. "I just want to get my daughter some help!" I exclaimed. "We're going to help her," they said, "but we are going to have to contact B.C.W. because that's abandonment." I hadn't the slightest idea of what B.C.W. was; neither did I know anything about the child welfare system. "Yeah, yeah. Whatever you say," I responded in frustration. They admitted Too Tough and contacted B.C.W. (Bureau of Child Welfare).

I stayed there with Too Tough for a long-time, feeling melancholy. I finally left and constantly returned to visit with her. Too Tough was teething; as a result, she had fevers and her ears bothered her. Word must have gotten to her mother because Victoria showed up at the hospital. I noticed she had gotten back with her little boyfriend again. I thought he was sporting a piece of jewelry I had given Victoria for Too Tough and I asked Victoria about it. She had developed what my little brother Nike called "selective amnesia"; she simply had no idea what I was speaking of.

Per the hospital's advice I filed a petition against the mother of my child. I was sort of placed in a catch-22 situation. Victoria was contacted, and we were sent for an interview in the family court at 161st St. in the Bronx. Victoria tried to degrade me in front of the interviewer; I guess she felt she'd get the baby back in this manner and all of the legal stuff would be over. She began with: "He is selling drugs, he is getting public assistance, he is working as a strip dancer, and super of a building!" The interviewer, who was a black woman, looked at Victoria and responded, "It sounds like he is doing good and can provide for her. Why are you telling me this? What are *you* doing?" Victoria was silent.

A short time thereafter we appeared before the family court judge. One of Victoria's girlfriends had told her to just say that the child isn't mine and the judge will automatically give her the baby. Open and shut case, right? Wrong! Not with this judge. The judge listened to this rhetoric and must have asked himself, w*hy would she all of a sudden claim that he isn't the father of the child?* The judge scheduled us to take a blood test and explained that with today's technologies all is needed is the mother, the child, and the father to determine paternity, and the test is very valid. Then came the moment of truth: would the judge give the child to the mother or to the father? If he could have looked inside my heart he would have known that I should remain with her because I had grown so attached to her. The judge said, "The child has been with the father and will remain with him for now."

I arrived downtown early with Too Tough for the blood test. We waited for some time, but Victoria never showed up, which had me puzzled. We returned to court on the next date. Victoria gave the court an excuse why she had not shown up for the blood test. The judge scheduled another date for the blood test to take place.

Again, I arrived downtown early with Too Tough for the test, and again Victoria did not show up. On the next scheduled return date, the judge was not trying to hear any excuses and made sure that this was understood. He told Victoria, "Ms. Doomis, if you are not there for the next scheduled blood test I am going to show you who run this court!"

By then, several months had passed since I had gotten bailed out and I was getting a little rabbit in me. I had too many cases open and the court system wanted some time out of me. There was no getting around it. I thought hard. I considered all my alternatives and possibilities, and I made the decision to give Victoria the baby. When we came out of the courtroom I walked over to Victoria with the baby in my arms and said, "I can't fight you anymore. I am going to go to jail. I am going to cop out and do some time." I then gave her the best part of me: my precious seed. We all left.

Victoria really wasn't a bad person and, as I think back, I wish that I had done better by and for her and my daughter. I loved Victoria in many ways. She was the first woman that I ever asked to marry me. We didn't get married, though. I think things weren't right and the timing just wasn't right either. What she may have lacked in certain areas she made up for in others. Whenever she gave herself freely it was like heaven, and I loved to watch her enjoy herself. It was at those times that I'd say she was a great lover. I am grateful to her for those precious moments and also for bearing my one and only biological child. There is no way to change the things that have been done because what is done is done. We had some good times and some bad times together. It is just unfortunate that it had to all end that way. I have not seen Victoria since that day and I have only seen Too Tough about three times since then. That was at least 11 years ago. It has been legally established that she is my daughter.

Samantha

Samantha Marie Monroe was her name. I met her after getting out of the Bronx House of Detention on bail. I had just lost my baby's mother to some p---y-licking slickster.

I can clearly remember the day Samantha and I met, as if it were yesterday. It was around 5:00 p.m. on a nice summer afternoon. I had gone to an "herb gate" to get a bag of reefer to smoke. This particular spot had a glass mirror as a partition. When I went to make the buy there she was waiting, willing to take my order.

Samantha wore sky blue, like the clouds above, and she sat high upon a chair, looking as proud as a queen. Her hair was out sexy-like, and when she smiled she flashed clean white teeth. Her eyes were the pretty big brown type and they sat well in her facial frame. Whether she was smiling at me or at the baby (who I had strapped to my chest), I really couldn't tell. However, I remember the smile and I remember that I wanted to order more than just the reefer at that point.

Samantha was 1/2 Black and 1/2 Puerto Rican. She was very fair-skinned in complexion, which we called "red bone." There was no doubt that she had caught my attention. "Hi! Let me get a nickel bag please," I asked her, while placing the money in the slot. I made my buy and exchanged a few words with her. She congratulated me on having a pretty baby. "Come and see me sometimes," I said. As I was walking out she called to me and said, "Hey! Are you going to tell me where to come see you at?" I was embarrassed, and then I smiled and told her that I lived up the block at 15-15 Macombs Road. "The people who own the building are like family, so all you have to do is ask for Shake." Actually, the owners were in-laws by common law marriage. During this time I was going back and forth to court for my cases, and I had just petitioned Victoria on abandonment charges.

About a week later I was walking and noticed Samantha and some guys smoking reefer in a park area where pigeons and old people came to cool out on the benches. I walked over to where she was and spoke with her as if she belonged to me. "Why haven't you been by?" I asked her. The question was more like a demand. She was startled at my approach and hesitated in her response. I looked at her associates as if to ask, "What do you have to do with this?" I said to her, "Yeah, well you know where I am." Then I kept walking, with my baby on my back. I thought nothing else of this.

The next day I had my daughter strapped to my chest, a shopping cart full of laundry and a big bag of laundry in my hand as well. I was on my way out of the building when Samantha stepped to her business. She actually flipped the script on me. She spoke to me as if I belonged to her or she had some type of authority. "Where are you going?" she asked. I smiled, both because I was surprised to see her and because she was a pretty sight to see. "I am going to the laundry," I said. "Give me the baby," she demanded. This was the beginning of our relationship.

Samantha was very pretty, but she was also very tough. She'd been through a lot, and she was very poor. She'd been seeing an older guy when we met. She left him in a heartbeat for me. Women!

While we were together, I noticed Samantha's actions were a little different than Victoria's. This was my second experience of living with a woman. Samantha was very good with Too Tough and she was very clean in the house in general. Victoria had been less likely to do housework than Samantha. I had never had a woman give me a massage or talk to me the way Samantha did. For example, Samantha would get the baby cream when I came out of the shower or bathtub, and she would lay me down and massage my body from head to foot. When she finished, she would say, "I want some sex." The problem was that those were the only words that she seemed to know: "Give me some sex." "I want some sex." Being that my body was relaxed, I was only 22 years old, and she had been fattening me up for the kill, I wasn't about to refuse. Besides, I never had many women and was really inexperienced at lovemaking. However, with Samantha there could always be something new; she seemed to know all of the tricks and positions. In fact, it was all new and fun to me. It was something to watch her operate; after a while, I just learned the magic words. I would say them like one would say "abracadabra": "Samantha, give me some sex, sugar." Boy, was that easy.

Victoria was moody sometimes and didn't want to be bothered. This made me upset, and I would have to rough off the sex by wrestling with her. Funny thing though, Victoria always seemed to be O.K. after that. It was almost as if it was a game she liked to play, and if I didn't play she would think that I didn't love her. She was talkative and everything, although she wasn't saying much of anything. Samantha, on the other hand, was always willing, ready, and able. She was a nymphomaniac. I don't remember her ever saying no to sex when we were together, and I don't remember her ever being on her period.

I started selling some weed again. I had just come home on bail and I was trying to get back on my feet. I did a few side jobs in the building, continued to get public assistance and danced at a club as a male strip dancer. With all of this, I was looking for more work. Those strip joints would have a different guy every other week or so.

Peter

Things seemed to start to move pretty quickly. I met a guy named Peter who had a connection to some angel dust juice. The juice was very good, and I told him that I could move it if he got it. Sure enough, he got the juice.

Much Better was one of the leading quality dusts out in 1982. The bag that it came in was stamped with an elephant tilting over, which symbolized the power of the drug (angel dust was said to be an elephant tranquilizer). I traced the stamp and had a rubber stamp made just like it. Once again, ingenuity came from a well of potential and a desire to succeed against all odds.

Peter asked me, "How are you going to use that stamp when that s--t ain't yours?" "Don't worry about it," I told him. I used to work for my man Nikky (a.k.a. Almond Head) selling Much Better. Now it was time to make some money for self. As long as the dust was quality like Much Better, which it was, we were good to go. F--k that. I sold for him; he was supposed to be my homeboy from way back. I had my own thing now, that's all.

The dust juice was a monster. We got some peppermint leaves from the Spanish bodega and some spray to kill the smell while we went to work like chemists in our laboratory, which was the kitchen. We also bought some bags the same color as the Much Better bags (lime green) and, last but not least, the inkpad to stamp the bags with. We baked the leaves to get rid of all the excess liquids. Then we weighed out about 2 ounces of leaves and poured the leaves into a big Helmann's Mayonnaise jar. After that, we measured 1 ounce of dust juice per every 2 ounces of leaves and poured that over the leaves in the jar. The leaves and the juice were shaken together real well and the jar was sealed as tight as we could get it. Then, it was put in the freezer to sit. Although we sprayed the house, you could smell the juice many flights up in the building.

Everywhere we went all we said was, "Much Better, Much Better, Much better," very rapidly. "You got Much Better?" the customer asked. "Let me see the stamp," and then they investigated the stamp. The stamp was very important, just as labels are on food products, clothing, etc. After looking at the label, the customers placed their order, which was anywhere from 1 to 75 bags, or more.

One of the reasons why some people bought so many bags is because people came from New Jersey, Long Island, Brooklyn, or some area that did not have the product. They usually bought a lot and sold the same bag for twice the amount where they came from.

There was one time that a dust patient (i.e., PCP addict) got angry because I wouldn't give him more products. He seemed to become psychotic. I first noticed him on the outside of the building; at the time, I didn't know that he had broken into my apartment. Some words were exchanged and some tussling occurred. All of a sudden, I found myself trying to get out of a headlock. He was a much bigger guy than I was. He kept hitting me in my back as he held my head in the lock. I didn't know it then, but he was blowing me up with a pair of scissors. He had gotten the scissors from out of the apartment (I used to keep a pair of scissors on top of a glass of water behind the door). I had heard that there was some sort of supernatural meaning to this, some power of protection.

After people noticed what was really happening and began to stir, the guy ran. Two minutes later, everyone was asking me, "Yo Shake, you alright?" I said, "Yeah, but I feel kind of sweaty on my back." I had on a very nice name-brand black leather jacket that I took off at that moment. All of a sudden somebody said, "Yo, Shake! You're bleeding like a motherf--ker." I looked at the blood and all the b---h came out of me. I started panicking and s--t. "Yo! Get a cab!" I yelled and nearly fainted.

Someone flagged a cab and I lay across somebody's lap as if I'd been shot with a shotgun. We went to Lebanon Hospital. I thought I was going to die. I don't know how, but my mother was there when they began the stitching. She told me how two of the stab wounds were less than one inch away from my spine.

I was moved to another hospital for recovery, and Samantha came to visit me there. I was in pain for a few days. Later, I could barely walk; it was a close call.

When I got out my friend G.G. gave me a long-length white rabbit coat that fit something proper and went well with my gear. I tried to keep up the rent and make sure the baby ate (while she was with me). At this time, Too Tough was with me daily; even as I scrambled I carried her on my chest.

Samantha used to hold the dust for me. I admired the fact that she seemed to be down with me no matter what. For this I would take her shopping and buy her anything her heart desired. She'd like a jacket and I'd get her flavors. Then I would say, "You need a pocketbook," "You need a hat," etc. and I'd buy them.

Once when I was in a restaurant with Samantha she began spoon-feeding me. We had ordered some West Indian food (I grew up on this type of food). She was the only woman besides my mother to do this. It was cute, I liked it, and it made me feel like a king. No person is all bad and there is some good in everyone, if we look for it.

Then something happened that I didn't expect. I received 50 quarters of heroin and was told, "Yo! Keep that." I was downtown in a pinstriped suit and some gray Pierre Cardin shoes when I got this package. The bag of quarters was placed in a brown paper bag and then placed on top of the counter. The party giving me the drugs said, "Yo! What are you going to do? Let the dope just sits there?" I didn't know that I had been hit until then. I bought some glycine bags, some tape, and a big cigar, and then I was set. "Taxi!" I yelled as I stepped out into the summer afternoon. I caught a cab and went back uptown to inform my homeboy Peter of the news. In my mind, it was on. This was the break that young kids who tried to get ahead in the drug game waited for.

Misunderstanding

Peter wasn't there when I returned. I saw my brother Stay High, who wasn't doing too well at the time. So I went in the freezer and gave him about 1/4 of an ounce of dust. "Take that, Arty, and do the right thing," I told him. I figured with 50 quarters of dope and all the dust we could stand it. Later on, Peter came with his girl Midnight. I told him what time it was: "Yo, I have got 50 quarters of some high-powered dope. We are on, baby. Oh, yeah."

I gave my little brother a little dust to get on his feet. We smoked a little dust and were bugging. When I got ready to bag up the dope, the s--t was gone. At the same time, I noticed Peter and his girl Midnight were leaving. Like a fool I started looking for the dope all over because the dust had me thinking slower than normal and imagining s--t. Peter had high-tailed it downtown in a cab with the dust and the dope. He had misunderstood my helping my brother as robbing him. This was the only thing I could conclude from his actions; he had never done anything like this before.

Peter wasn't a dope seller so he gave the dope to Motor, my other brother's friend, to sell. Motor and Leonard sold a lot of drugs together on 116th St. and Lenox Avenue in front of the Jimmy Daniels bar. I had gotten this information about Motor having gotten the drugs from Peter by simply asking around. I started to sober up and think straight and s--t started to come together.

I went to Peter's house with Samantha. I asked him about the dope and he insisted that he didn't have it and he didn't know what happened to it. Somehow I managed to find the bag of dust he had stashed. While he wasn't looking, I got it and threw it out the window into the backyard where all the garbage was, and then I rushed out of his crib. There I was on the stairs of 114th St. between St. Nicholas and 8th

Avenue, across the street from Wadleigh School. Peter came downstairs, right behind me. We were both standing on the stoop, there were bright lights, and the people were selling drugs a hundred miles an hour. All of a sudden, the police pulled up and grabbed me and left Peter. They searched me and found about 10 bags of dust on me. They took me in.

While in the precinct, the police kicked me in my testicles, one of their favorite pastimes. They came back from the lab with a report stating that I had some sort of vegetable substance on me, and they let me go.

Samantha was right there waiting. We hopped into a cab and went right back to Peter's. I was hoping he hadn't found the bag of dust. I told Samantha to hold the cab and I would be right back. "Don't ask no questions," I told her, "just hold the cab." I had the cab park around the corner with the engine running. I ran back to the building and went into the backyard. I didn't have to search for long, as the smell of the dust was so strong that all I had to do was to follow my nose. I smiled from ear to ear when moments later I found the bag full of dust. I grabbed the bag and hurried back to the cab. "Let's go," I told the cab. "Where to?" he asked. "123rd St. and 1st Avenue." I was going to pay Mr. Motor, who lived in Wagner Projects, a visit.

I showed Samantha the dust as the cab pulled away from the curb into the middle of the darkness. I was feeling better. I had Samantha knock on the door and ask for Motor. Motor answered the door. Once I heard his voice, I yelled, "Yo, come out! I want to talk to you!" Motor came out trying to play it off like everything was everything, although he knew exactly what was going down. I lured him away from the front of his door and quickly snatched him up by the collar and asked him, real serious-like, "Where's my f----g dope, nigger?" He began explaining, "Yo, man, Peter gave it to me."

Motor had filled up his mother's refrigerator with steak and other food. I made him turn over all the rest of the dope that he had. He claimed that he had spent all the money. I wasn't complaining, though, because I had started from nothing a few hours ago; now I held both bags (i.e., the dope and the dust).

I saw Peter a few days later, and we talked as if nothing had happened because we both knew and understood the unspoken language; there were no hard feelings. We walked to Central Park, and we sat on a big bolder and talked. He said to me, "One day we'll tell our kids about all of this." He had a son and I had a daughter.

Drugs and Addiction

It is important to mention that being an addict and having a constant supply of my favorite drugs kept me in a state of high. That is to say, my system stayed full of drugs. I was high literally from the time I got up to the time I went to bed. Even if I didn't smoke or sniff anything upon awakening in the morning, I had a system full of drugs and was basically high. Once, my brother Stay High had smoked so much dust for such a long period of a time that he actually fell out in the hallway. He had been hanging out with some get-high partners, and when he awoke he realized that they had robbed him and left him.

This whole thing about angel dust and drugs in general was and is still devastating to both the individual user and the families of those who use. If you ever want to know how it affects a family, you should speak with my mother. I remember one time my brother Adam had smoked some angel dust. He looked like he was going to kill everybody in the house. He scared the s--t out of me. I tried to hurry up and get him some milk because milk would bring down the dust high. I could only imagine what my mother must have been feeling to see three of her sons (Adam, Stay High, and me) smoking that s--t. Even my sister smoked it. I figure that it must have been devastating for her because she used to say that she'd rather see us strung out on heroin than that goddamned dust. It is a miracle we all survived that plague.

Any addict can probably tell you a different story about his or her involvement with drugs. It may be difficult to understand what they've gone through. I'll tell you, it isn't really a nice thing and all the get-high is not worth losing all that you lose. Ask Spencer Haywood (famous basketball player), Thomas Henderson (famous Dallas football player), or the parents of those who become hooked on this deadly disease that catches you in its web and refuses to let you go. In the coming years, I will end up losing my wife and my freedom as a direct result of the drugs I craved. However, in my mind I saw it quite differently. I was never wrong about anything; it was always somebody else.

One day I looked up and Samantha had begun to sniff a lot of coke. Eventually, she started to flip on me. I found out that she was seeing someone else, who was in prison, while I was trying to give her the world. I had heard this through the grapevine; my mind had been in a maze and I had seen only what I wanted to see.

One day I went to get her from her friend's apartment so that we could spend some time together. I'd heard that she was planning a visit to Rikers Island. All this time it had never occurred to me that I had anything to do with possibly chasing her away. As far as I was concerned, as long as I provided her with drugs and money, what the f--k, she should have no complaint. So, I continued on with my illusions and never thought about what it was I should be really providing my woman with. Things like responsibility, devotion, and loyalty crossed my mind, but they never really took root.

I decided to go and try to speak with Samantha about the situation. I figured I would just go get her and take her home and try to make things right because she was out of order. She was wrong and things were wrong all because of her. I told myself that it was all because of her.

I knocked on the door of the place where she had stayed that night; it was about 6:30 a.m. in the winter. Ms. Joyce's mother Laverne came to the door and I asked her for Samantha. She got Samantha but Samantha didn't even want to speak. I pleaded with her to come with me, but her heart was hardened. I had two 32-caliber pistols on me. There I was: angry as hell at myself, my addiction, at the world, and at the system that had its hooks in me. I had no way to release my anger. All of the things that should have been there as support systems for guys like me were not there. I don't know exactly what should have been there, only that I wish there had been something there for me then. I was now a second felony offender and a bill was about to be passed that says three times and you are in for life. Lord, have mercy on us victims.

I got off some shots right there in the hallway to sort of let Samantha know that she was going to make me kill her if she kept it up. I became very frustrated and went out and committed another robbery, with money already in my pocket. In retrospect, I must have been tired and upset really with myself. I remember it as if it were yesterday.

Grand Larceny, Robbery,
and
Attempted Homicide

I was dressed in $300 soft Italian leather dark blue boots with low-cut heels and long round-pointed-toes. I wore dark blue Oscar de la Renta corduroys, and a thick white winter sweater. My hair was in a style called "S curls," which cost me $35. I wore a 3/4-length unisex raccoon coat that was spotted brown. I had two guns, a pocket full of money, and a heart full of frustration and anger.

I stormed out the building after shooting up in the ceiling, only to pace the streets in the wee hours of the morning. Although I wasn't looking for trouble, if the opportunity presented itself there would be trouble. At this point, I was a menace to society and to myself. I only hope that when guys who have actually been classified as menaces to society come up with some rational ideas for solutions that they will at least be listened to. I don't know if the prison system really addresses this problem, but I can understand the need for something.

As I was crossing the street at Mt. Eden and Jerome Avenue, where the cars come up off the Major Deegan Expressway, I spotted what appeared to be a vic. There was this big flashing diamond ring, a large gold heart with diamond studs, and a white lady with an unlocked car door. It was about 8:00 a.m. She was probably on her way to work or on her way home to her family.

Without hesitation or a second thought, I snatched the car door open and drew my gun. I snatched the gold heart with the diamond studs in it and told her to give me the diamond ring. She started yelling, which only made me act anxiously. I snatched her out of the car and in the process a shot went off, the bullet hitting the ground. The lady fled as if running for her life. She fell down and scraped her knee on her own, while running in fear.

I jumped in the car and sped away. I made three left turns and parked the car in front of my building. I went in and changed my clothes, leaving my guns, the gold piece, and some money on the table. After a minute or two, I figured, "What the hell, the car is a brand new Monte Carlo. Maybe I could have my Spanish friends strip it. Maybe I could then get an old body and put the new engine inside." So I stepped outside and began to speak with a neighbor of mine about my idea. While I was talking to him the police pulled up and jumped out of the car with their guns drawn. I knew I didn't fit any description because I had changed into a white sweatshirt and some sky blue pants.

"I didn't do it," my neighbor yelled. "He told me he just wanted to get the new engine from a car he stole." I was then taken and I.D.'d on the spot. I was taken in and charged with attempted homicide, grand larceny, and assault. I was out on bail for a robbery, and I was on interned supervision for a Y.O. (youthful offender) robbery. The next time I would see the street would be in six years. I hope one day to be able to meet my victims on different terms and apologize publicly to them all. Thank God there weren't that many, but then one is too many.

State Senator and Friend JB

State Senator JB represented me, on a pro-bono basis. I had already known him from when I had helped in one of his campaigns. I therefore had a chance to meet and see him face to face.

I was given a 7:30 a.m. examination, which is a tactic used to stall for time. I was sent to Bellevue Hospital where I met a lot of different people with many different personalities. Many of them were not in the least bit crazy. I observed firsthand how prisoners who had mental problems were treated. For the most part, the hospital staff did not seem to care in the least: guys would be in the bathroom having sex with some poor guy on the regular who really didn't know any better because he had the mind of a child though his chronological age may have been 21 years old. They had one guy who used to write weird letters to women, which may have been his way of getting attention. Here you have some guys who have committed murders, robberies and assaults all together with guys who have something as simple as some obsessive-compulsive disorder.

I was given psychotropic medications that I have yet to see the possible full aftereffects of and underwent different psychological testing. They asked me questions like, "Who was the first president?" I would respond by saying something like, "The pink elephant on the motorcycle." I was willing to do anything to get out of doing the time they were talking about, which was at least 9 to 27 years. I used to slobber all over myself in front of nurses, and even literally jumped on the table and pulled out my penis in front of one of them. Sometimes, while I was in my cell at night in Rikers Island, I would scream at the top of my lungs and go under the bed, where the police would find me when they arrived. They would go get the nurse and I would say that there was a big flying rabbit inside of the cell. They would take me out to the hospital after that or place me in an observation unit. The saddest part of this whole ordeal was having my mother and fiancée come to visit me there and telling them that everything was going to be all right.

I learned how to play the card game pinochle with two Spanish guys. We played that game from the time we got up to the time we went to bed. The meals were much better there in Bellevue. We used to get snacks and different types of dips with some celery sticks.

Some of the peculiar behaviors that I observed while I was there: one guy used to be only allowed out at certain times because he was very violent. He would be sitting next to you eating and all of a sudden, for no reason, he would just haul off and punch you upside the head and fight with you. Security put him back in the cage when he did this. A lot of the other guys used to just walk back and forth, smoking cigarettes, in a small area for hours. Back and forth, back and forth, back and forth. Once in a while they would stop and look out the window because the unit we were in allowed us to see into the street.

None of the things I did worked; tricks only worked for guys like J.J. Hinckley, who only needed to say he was stressed. He would take some aspirin and their effects would leave him hallucinating. But those of us who smoked angel dust, which really puts you out of touch with reality, were always found competent to stand trial.

Meanwhile, I went back and forth to court with Senator JB. I liked Mr. JB. It was something to see the white men in the courtroom giving him the respect they did. The judge, as well as most of the others, would address him as Senator JB. I ended up receiving one year for the youthful offense, 4 to 12 years for the attempted murder, grand larceny and robbery, and 2 to 6 years for the robbery. There had been no attempted homicide, but I had to plea to it in order to get the deal that was offered to me. The Senator took me as far as he could, but he told me that he would not take this to trial with me.

While lying up on Rikers Island and waiting to go upstate, I noticed a lot of changes from when I'd been on the Island in the early seventies. For example, brothers didn't have one-on-one fights anymore. A Brooklyn mob might jump and stomp out a Manhattan brother, or vice versa. In addition, a whole posse would hold down a jack (i.e., a telephone). If a guy was down with the strong crew in the jail and moved into a housing unit he would ask, "Yo! Whose jack is this?" If he'd already cased the spot and felt he was strong enough or had enough manpower, he would do a takeover. He would just take the jack out of the socket and say, "This f----g jack is mine. If anybody has a problem with this, see me in the back." He would definitely have his burner (i.e., knife) on him and possibly his posse on the side with their burners in case s--t got funky. If nobody said anything, the phone was his. However, sometimes guys would let him do this and wait until night, when it was real dark, and they would blow his a-- out of the frame and send him out leaking. To blow meant to rip him with razors or stab him with knives; to leave leaking was to be bleeding. It was not unusual to see guys leaving out leaking out of the sides of their face from a fresh New York razor or a fresh New York 007 blade that may have come in via an officer who was down with one of the prison gangs, or an officer who was a family member of a prisoner.

Some guys would say, "Don't play yourself on the jack or you'll get a buck 50." "A buck 50" meant 150 stitches from a fresh razor, usually across the face. If a guy cut a guy real bad, the rest of the guys down with this would give him praise or props by saying, "Yo, you did marvelous work to that nigger." This is why I believe we as a people are regressing. This attitude doesn't just develop in or stay in the jails. We are a lost people, confused, lashing out blindly in the wind. We are constantly missing our marks. Our rite of passage comes from whatever the fad is and has no structure. I don't want to sound pessimistic, rather tell how I see the situation now.

During the rest of the six years I went to school, earned my GED, and went to many drug and behavior modification programs. I even began college. I stayed out of trouble and maintained family ties, with the exception of my daughter because the maternal grandmother refused to even consider helping me. I would not see my daughter for six years, and for six years I would reflect and hope for the day that I would be free and could see her again. It would not be easy to beat the court system, as I was able to see from my rough introduction to them. It was going to be a rough ride. Senator JB did not wish to take the cases to trial. He had all of the little charges run concurrent with the larger ones, and then he relieved himself of the cases.

Rough Riding

.   I decided to begin to get myself together because I obviously was not going home any time soon. I signed up for school, I took the GED, and I decided to get married to Samantha. Actually, I had wanted to marry her before coming to jail; the question had been asked, but we just never got around to it. The most we had done was look at some rings.

February 13, 1984: on my daughter's second birthday a loud voice rang through the cellblocks at approximately 5:00 a.m., "Alright! Listen up! Grayling Ferrand, pack it up, you're going upstate." I was up already and anxious to go because I'd heard so much about upstate, in the mountains where the big boys went. It was customary for prisoners to give away all the things they had accumulated in the city jail because they couldn't take anything with them upstate, except maybe soap and cosmetics (even this is not permitted nowadays).

After being processed, I was shackled with chains around my waist, handcuffs on my wrist, and leg cuffs on my ankles. I felt very uncomfortable, and I was reminded me of the slave movies I'd seen like Roots. It was almost if they were locking up Fort Knox. I was then thrown into a big bus along with a lot of other black men.

As the big greyhound bus left Elmhurst, Queens (Rikers Island prison) and headed to Downstate Correctional Facility, I remained silent and my mind was a blank. I went to sleep and before I knew it, we were there in Fishkill, New York. Once we stepped into the facility, the s--t began. They placed us in a square room, and the initiation began: "Alright! Listen Up!" one of the white officers yelled. In the background, a black man stood out as a token; one could not tell if he was a black man trying to make a living or a Negro trying to lap up the white man's a--. In another place, you could hear another black man, but his voice was responding to the pain that was being inflicted upon him. He was being made an example, as they did the slaves who rebelled on the slave ships (i.e., some of the slaves who rebelled were said to have been thrown overboard to the sharks). The goon squad emerged from the room where the poor man must have been still moaning in pain. These guards emerged with smiles and laughed about the whole thing. It was normal practice for the guards to use excessive force. The officer doing the orientation allowed us to observe the incident briefly and then he brought us back to attention by saying, "You are my property now and you'll do as you are told! Does anybody have a problem with what I am saying? Because if so, we can straighten it out the way we just straightened the guy in there out."

All around me were a bunch of guys that looked alike. They had sticks and uniforms to help make them look tough; the officer continued, "Everybody take everything out of your pockets and place it on the bench. Turn around, facing the wall with your hands on the wall. Kick off your shoes, shut your mouth and wait for instructions." Anybody who didn't follow instructions, whether he understood them or not, was beat down.

The next thing they did was strip us. We were made to strip off all our clothes and expose our anal cavity to these officers on command. The officers seemed to enjoy looking inside a man's a--hole. Sick! Then we were forced to cut all our hair off our heads and faces. We were forced to cut our fingernails, wash up with some liquid solution, and then wear state-issued prison uniforms. The guards all seemed to be trying to get revenge for the Attica riot where officers were forced to feel some of the pain, dehumanization, and deprivation prisoners were forced to endure everyday. It is enough punishment just having to serve six years.

I was then placed in a reception unit. I was allowed one phone call (collect), three meals, and one hour of recreation. I had to stand for the head count four times a day. I later took several psychological tests and listened to a lecture on drugs. I became interested in drug counseling and was allowed to speak about angel dust. Ms. Storm thought I had a natural ability to kick it live, so I was allowed to speak at other orientations.

I received one visit while there. My mother came along with some people who I called in-laws (my sister was living with a man with whom she had bore a son). Two things were learned from that visit which would help me for the duration of this prison term: 1) my mother told me to just reflect over my past. I did and I realized how much money must have gone through my hands. I realized that my mother tried to do her best and I realized more about myself and the knowledge of who I'd been and who I had become, which are not necessarily things I'm able to articulate verbally. The essence of my existence transcends any finite explanation of who I was, where I came from, or where I was at that time. Many more things were learned while reflecting in that cell. It helped me just to reflect. Mama may not have a college education, but she has wisdom 2) my sister's man at the time, Heave, had come to see his brother G.G. and he came over to my table said, "Hold your head." He probably didn't think anything more of it. However, I remembered this my whole prison term. I literally had to hold my head in dealing with some correctional officers who were a--holes and prisoners who acted just as bad, if not worse.

From Downstate Correctional Facility I went to Sing Sing Correctional Facility and was stationed in the transit block. I was given recreation practically all day. The result of my GED test came back, and since I was tired of so much recreation, I decided to continue in a school program. I went to pre-college and earned a couple of certificates upon whose completion I signed up for Mercy College. I also began boxing.

So far things seemed to be pretty routine, until one day when coming in from the yard I noticed a shadow hiding on the side. It felt like someone evil was there. A minute later somebody was hit (i.e., stabbed) in the eye; he lost that eye. I don't know what it was about, and I didn't try to find out because one of the golden rules in prison is "mind your business."

I wrote as many as 15-20 letters a week; I might have gotten one response back. Nobody seemed to like to write and still don't. I didn't receive any visitors, and my wife seemed to be another one to add to my list of shattered dreams. Sometimes I would write to everybody that I could think of. Over the year I would learn to express myself, though. My spelling was atrocious and my writing may not have met the dominant culture's standard. The most important thing I find that came out of all of that is the practice helped me to develop even to the point of being able to write this book. I would develop my writing skills to the point that I could take a word and write a song, a poem, or an essay about it. I could take seminal ideas and write a book from just that.

After the college semester, I was P.K.'d (i.e., transferred) to Auburn Correctional Facility. I attended religious services a lot there, both Muslim and Christian. I often conversed with the 5% Nation and eventually joined them. I found their views and philosophy to be more real than most others I had learned about. The only concept I had problems with was the idea that all white people were devils. "Come on! You've got to be kidding. That is absurd to think that all white people are devils," I would say. They would get very hot with me and say that I was acting like the devil because I didn't simply conform as most did. My understanding of some of the lessons was different as well, thus the result was too much confusion. I simply would not take on face value what I was being taught. In short, I stopped professing to be a 5%er, but I kept the name that I had chosen for myself, which meant "Love, Truth, Peace, Freedom and Justice, Allah" ("Justice" for short). These names came from the five principles of the Moorish Science Temple of America.

I signed up for the college program there in Auburn. The name of the college was Cayuga, and I did fairly well. I also signed up for the boxing team there. I worked out with Joe Black, Kasin, and a guy named Biscuit. My institutional program was to work in the bakery. One day while on break in the bakery I wrote a poem entitled "Free my people."

Not two weeks after I arrived in Auburn, somebody was hit bad in the mess hall. The prison was shut down; the guy probably died. The officers fed us out of paper bags.

I stayed in Auburn for one year. I didn't see my wife at all while I was there. I even sent her $200 to come up on the trailer visit, but she didn't even say thank you. The drug bee of society had bitten her: crack was on the move.

I believe I received two visitors despite the fact that the transportation was free. My brother Stay High surprised me by coming up. He showed me the vial that the new drug was placed in and he told me how bad (i.e., good) it was. To this day, ten years later, that drug has my brother fighting like hell for freedom from its grip. In his case, too, crack was on the move, irrespective of person. It was, nevertheless, a pleasure to see Stay High, even though it was obvious from his appearance that he was not doing very well. I believe the other visit I received was from my sister.

After a year in Auburn, I was told that I was going to Green Haven because of good behavior. In Green Haven, I enrolled in Marist College, signed up for the boxing team, and took music as an institutional program. I liked music. I earned several certificates and became a teacher's assistant in music theory. I learned to read and write music, and I learned to play the piano. I trained with Sharrif from the singing group, "The Escorts", from New Jersey. They cut a record called, *Three Down and Four to Go*. One of their hit records was entitled, *Lets Make Love at Home Sometimes*.

Some of the people that I trained in with in boxing were: La Tel, Big Earl China (280 pounds solid), and the Boxing Commissioner Tricky Trick, who later turned Muslim in Green haven. My boxing improved, but I began to realize that I was nearing the time to meet with the parole board, and I began to consider exactly what they would want. I didn't think that they would consider boxing very highly, so I dropped boxing and focused more on the things that I felt would help increase my chances of getting out at the earliest possible date. By then I was almost three years away from the parole board since my arrest in 1983.

In my spare time I played piano in shows and in church, and I sang background for the choir. I read a lot of books in my spare time as well. I read books like George Jackson's *Soledad Brothers* and *Blood in My Eye*. I read Malcolm X's autobiography, and all of Donald Goines' books.

Things seemed to be going so-so. I still hadn't received any visits from my wife, but my sister started visiting me. Once she left $500 in my account. All heads used to turn when she visited me because she wore the finest of silk dresses, mink coats, and nice jewelry. She also drove up in an expensive car, a brand-new up-to-date BMW.

I smoked reefer to help ease the pain I felt from being incarcerated. All of a sudden my past caught up with me: someone who knew me when I had gone through my phase of sexual mis-identity, spotted me and labeled me. Before long those who hung out with me started to ask me, "Yo, Shake. What's up, man? Motherf--kers talking about you and stuff." I was never much for lying or being a plastic individual. I saw the look of sincerity in my homeboys' faces when they asked the question. I was embarrassed, but I had too much pride to lie. "It's like this: I began when I was younger in the adolescent joint. I went through an experience like that, but I ain't with that and I am not gay." Although my homeboys understood, my story only confirmed the rumor. "Yeah, he was down with that s--t, so he must be gay." I was propositioned at least twice in a joking manner. At that time, Green

Haven had 879 lifers and the majority was serving time for sexual offenses. I was forced to perform orally once when I was caught in a dark shower with soap in my hair and face. It hurt me to get caught out there like that, but it was more like having been stuck up because I had done this before. I believe that if this would have been a first time it would have had a more devastating effect.

Another incident comes to mind from Green Haven: there was a guy named Philly Dee who had robbed some Spanish kid for a gold chain. He pretended to be all right with me until one day he tried to play me. "Yo! Get me this when you go to the store," he said to me. "What?" I asked. "I ain't getting s--t," I told him. Then he pulled some s--t out that looked like a New York 007 knife. He poked me in my hand, and the knife cut my skin. I slammed my cell gate closed and began thinking, *what the f--k do I do now?* I had decided about two years ago to stay out of trouble and to get out of that prison. At that moment, I was not sure if I wanted to change up my strategy.

The officer came around later and asked if I wanted to go to eat or to yard rec. I refused both. Phil came by my cell telling me, "Yo, I was just kidding and f----g with you. You can come out 'cause I ain't going to f--k with you." I wanted to blow this motherf--ker's brains to smithereens. I didn't answer him, and I didn't come out because I was afraid. I didn't have a knife, and if I did have one, I didn't want a body. No, I wanted to go home. A few other guys spoke with me, and I came out later the next day. I believe that Philly Dee had heard about my sister's boyfriend from someone in the joint and decided that he should back off because maybe something would happen to him if I were seriously hurt.

A couple of days later I moved to the west side of the prison, which was a breather. I stayed on the west side about one year then I became eligible for a medium facility and was transferred to Washington Comstock.

Washington Comstock didn't have a four-year college program, so I learned janitorial maintenance. I earned a couple of certificates that enabled me to make higher pay. I earned about $20 every two weeks. Basically, I just kept the dormitory clean. The medium facilities are not like the maximums A's that have all cells; mediums have dorms. Moe, my homeboy from the Foster Projects, was there. Moe had done about eight years in jail. We were the same age, and both of us had grown up staying in trouble and spending most of our time in some sort of prison.

I spent my spare time in the music room, and I exercised. The heavy bag, speed bag, and running were my way of relieving stress. Ironically, as one gets closer to the time for the parole board, the more stress one feels.

About ten months later I went to Fishkill Facility, where I became the Public Relations Chairman for the NAACP there. I joined the music program and taught music theory. I later joined the Network program. I did well in the program until somebody who'd heard from somebody else that they heard I was gay in Green Haven. While in a group discussion, he brought this issue up and asked me was I ever gay. "Hell no!" was my response. "That's not what I heard in Green Haven," he said. Then he asked, "Are you calling me a liar?" And there I was, in a hot seat amongst some homeboys and other hardened criminals. "I'm not gay!" I told him. By then I was about 1 1/2 years to the parole board.

About two weeks later, I came down the stairs from building 21. It was dark at the landing, and as I stepped off the last stairs I stepped into an ambush. "Bam!" I was caught on the top of my head with some sort of object. Like a fish that tries to get loose from a hook in its mouth, I went left, right, forward, and backward in an attempt to get away from the immediate danger. "O! O!" I yelled like a natural b---h. My scream opened a path for me, and I jetted through it. While coming up out of that area, I hit my left shoulder against a wooden beam. The impact caused me to get a jolt to the left side of my neck, and I became semi-paralyzed in that area. I had to let my left arm just hang as I walked to help ease the pain on my neck.

The police arrived and asked me what happened. "I don't know. Some guys tried to jump me and I hurt myself." I was so close to going home, I had one year left. *F--k it*, I told myself, *I am not going to let anything stop me from going home.*

My sister had stopped coming to see me because crack had claimed her soul too. I signed up for involuntary protective custody, which is a no-no in jail, but f--k it. I wasn't trying to deal with the peer pressure; I wanted to go home, and I was becoming older and wiser. In my opinion, I was doing the right thing.

About two months later I was shipped to Otisville State Correctional Facility. I again taught music theory, got involved with drug counseling programs, and just tried to stay out of trouble. I didn't receive any visitors or letters while there.

I was denied work release, so I figured I wasn't going to make it out, any way you buy it. But then, Albany took a careful look at my institutional records, and after a careful inspection, they considered me to be okay to be released. One evening, when mail was being given out, my name was called. I was given an envelope that came from Albany. Enclosed was an earned eligibility certificate. This meant that someone in Albany recognized I was about to meet with the parole board. Basically, this meant that as far as Albany was concerned I met the minimum requirements to be considered for release. It was sort of their stamp of approval.

Sure enough, time passed and I met with the parole board. I didn't really know what I was supposed to say. I just showed them all my certificates and sat there looking stupid and waiting for their lead.

After a while I received another white envelope telling me I was to meet with some people who would give me their decision. The decision was positive: I had made the board. Damn! I didn't believe it, and I actually felt as if I was given something other than a natural thing, something that I should have had already: freedom. Only man locks up animals and themselves.

I was later sent to Lincoln Correctional Facility to await my release. While there I met a homeboy named Essey. This guy sang like a canary. We got together and got access to the piano and made a few nice songs.

Mona lived next door to Lincoln; since she was like family she brought me salmon cakes, grits, and eggs for breakfast. We were allowed to have cooked foods there because we were going home anyway. I understand that they used to allow cooked foods in all the facilities until drugs started popping up in the chickens.

My sister Elaine came on the morning I was to be released, to pick me up. She looked no more than 10 pounds, as if she were an anorexic. But she was there, with the look of sisterly love in her eyes, and I loved her for just being there.

I stepped out of the door on January 3, 1989. I had not seen the streets in six years: no Christmas, New Year or Thanksgiving outside of prison. Though I stepped out the door, I was only free in part; I immediately had to go to see my assigned parole officer. *Was I really free?* I wondered.

Six Months Run

After seeing my parole officer and listening to his threats, I attempted to make contact with my daughter. I called her grandmother and she seemed a little shocked to find that I was home. Anyway, she told me that I'd have to make arrangements if I wanted to see my daughter. I thought she was crazy and I was very upset when she told me this, but prison had taught me a little patience. "O.K." I said, "How can I make these arrangements?" "Call me back Sunday," she demanded.

I called her Sunday, and she had her husband answer the telephone. "What is it?" he asked. "Hello sir, I am calling to make arrangements to see my daughter per your wife's instructions." He responded, "Well, you have to see the baby's mother if you want to see Too Tough." It almost sounded like a rehearsed response. "What do you mean I have to see Victoria? I have not seen Victoria in six years and I have no idea where she is." "Well," he said, "Victoria don't live here. Don't call here any more." Bang! The phone went dead. I wondered what could I do now. If I became angry or aggressive, they would simply call my parole officer and tell him. The parole officer would probably come and arrest me. The parole officers usually call certain people in the community and tell them to let them know if there is any problem: "We are releasing Grayling back to the community, a robber," etc. The police are notified of this and it is the easiest way to trap a black ex-con back into the system. I think this may have a lot to do with the 85% recidivism rate.

In my mind, the only way to get respect and to be able to be recognized as a father, etc., was to catch up on all those things I had lost. If I could just get a nice car, nice apartment, etc., I would be able to see my daughter regularly. In my mind, this was the American way. Materialistic? Yes.

Since the grandmother refused to let me see my daughter, I had to ask the uncle to sneak Too Tough out of the house. It was very beautiful just to see her for a few minutes.

Daddy's Little Girl

I was sitting downstairs in front of his building (his mother had gone to work). I was nervous and anxious to see my baby. I imagined that she must have been the same way. Finally, I saw them coming out of the building. I don't think I will ever forget those moments.

They came over to me, and my daughter and I just looked at each other. I saw deep pain in her eyes that said, *why? Where have you been? I missed you. I needed you. I have been through so much emotionally just thinking about you, daddy.* I also saw deep love that only a little girl has for her father. There were all of these feelings in her eyes at one time. It is sort of like when someone says, "I saw her age ten years, right before my eyes." I saw so many things in that split second. We just embraced each other as if we had spent those six years together and had never parted. I mean, she was just as happy and smiling with me as if she had known me all of her little life. It was a miracle what we felt. I think that this type of resilience is a part of some of the positive things that we have incorporated from the negative conditions we as a people had to endure during slavery. Before long, though, her uncle said, "Yo, Gee" (that's what he called me), "I have to get Too Tough back before my old earth comes back." "What did you call her?" I asked him, because I never called her Crystal, but rather Too Tough. "Oh, we call her Too Tough," he said.

Reunited

After I got out, I decided to go and find out what was up with my wife; I had questions I needed answered. I needed to know why she left me upstate all alone for six years. I had just gotten some clothes and I was pretty well dressed. I had on one of those sweaters with the padded shoulders, tiger skin and other designs. The sweater cost me nearly $100. I also had gotten some new footwear, pants, and a Kango hat. I had some money in my pocket and I was off to see if I could find Samantha.

I went to College Avenue and asked for my homeboy G-man. He wasn't hard to find because he was still trying to hustle. When he heard who was looking for him, he came out of the spot to greet me. I asked him had he seen my wife. For a minute, he didn't know of whom I was talking about. I refreshed his memory, and he immediately said with surprise, "Oh, yeah! I'll go get her for you." Samantha was right there in the spot, either working, hanging out, getting high, or lord knows what.

I wanted to cry when I saw her because this was not the wife I had left behind. Even though she had gotten high before with me, she never looked that bad. Those six years had done a lot to her. What on earth had she been through? Samantha had become a crack head. She had never smoked crack when I was home in 1982 because it really hadn't out. She looked like a gas station dog that is always dirty and you just kick when you go by if he approaches you.

Samantha came out, and when she saw me she immediately began bragging to her friends around her, "This is my husband. My husband just came home. This is the one I was telling you about." She grabbed hold of my coat, and I kissed her on her cheek, in pity and in love. I have never found it easy not to love a woman, as ironic as it may appear. "How have you been? Where is the family?" I asked her. "Come on," she said.

We walked up the block and went to her mother's house. Her mother was very cordial and polite and she loved me very much as a son-in-law. I think it's because neither of us can forget the first time we met and Samantha had said something disrespectful in front of her mother at the time she introduced me. I had immediately put that s--t in check and told Samantha she'd better not ever speak that way to her mother again. I had forgotten her mother was there. It was something I had learned from my mother: one should not disrespect their mother. I received too many whippings not to know this. If mom said shut up and you were just beaten, you should shut up and stop crying.

Samantha and I made love that night and I decided to give us a chance. I found it strange that she had learned certain things that she didn't know when I had left, but she was a pro at now. I will just say that it is a type of sexual favor.

I encouraged Samantha to join a rehab center, as I had been clean for six years while in jail. She seemed to try for a while, but I noticed that when I wasn't around she relapsed. I would have to come home and go look for her. I would eventually find her in some hallway getting high. Even if she tried to hide, she couldn't because I knew too many people who would tell on her. Many of her friends saw that I was trying, and they wanted her to get herself together. They only wished that they had a man who was as handsome and drug free, and was trying to help them.

One day, while cleaning up in Samantha's little room, I found some stale bloody Kotex in a box. She was unkempt, ill dressed, and she seemed to have done a complete 180°. I just sat there thinking, *this is not the Samantha that I knew.* Samantha had always been very clean and neat. Then one day I found a crack pipe of hers, and I told her that she was going to have to make a choice between the pipe and me. This was not a smart move. Samantha became almost hysterical and snatched her pipe from me. She made it clear that her pipe was important.

From then on, I began to stray away from Samantha. I had just come home from doing six years; I really wasn't able to have Samantha, so I took the easiest lay that I could find. I ended up catching the claps (i.e., gonorrhea). I told Samantha because I had made love to her a couple of times. I didn't want her to walk around with that disease (on top of the other one) and not know. Hence, we both went to the doctor. I still don't know who gave me the disease. When we left the hospital, Samantha became irritable and volatile. We argued, and she cursed me in the street. I couldn't stand for a woman to curse me in the street and told her to cool it. She persisted, and I slapped her. Samantha had always been a fighter, so when she began fighting me I had to calm her down by throwing her down on the ground, and out of uncontrolled anger I kicked her in the stomach.

I left that day, although it hurt me to do so. I told her that it was too hard for me to try to get on my feet with her pulling me down. I later found out that she was pregnant with our first child, something that she had always wanted from me.

While I was away I managed to begin to get things together. I went back to check on Samantha, but she was in jail for selling drugs. I didn't take advantage of the opportunity to help her, but rather I thought of the years she had left me upstate all alone. I wish I hadn't been bred in a society that was so bent on revenge because things might have worked out for the better. She called me on the phone and asked me for a visit. I declined. That was the gist of our reunion. I have not seen her since.

Trying the Traditional Way

The first job interview I went for was at a Roy Rogers agency. I was dressed up and got there very early in the morning. I was the first one. Finally, people came in and I sat before someone for an interview. "How are you?" asked the interviewer. "I am fine. I just need a job," I told him, straight out. Well, the only thing I can remember about that interview after that point is when he asked, "Do you have any arrests?" I responded, "Yes, sir. I have just been released from prison." His last words to me were, "O.K. We'll have our personnel manager contact your parole officer. Next!" The guy behind me was not well dressed at all, but he got a job.

Meanwhile, I was working voluntarily with some youth on 110th St. I liked working there; basically all I did was talk about some of the devastating effects of prison. I talked about some alternatives to prison, as well. It was easy because all I had to do was keep it real, which I did. They would come to me after the group discussion, out of the earshot of the staff, and tell me things like, "Yo! My brother is in Attica," or, "I have an uncle who was in Green Haven." They would ask me things about prison, and I would just tell them what I knew. While doing this volunteer work, I was trying to get access back into the prison system to speak with the brothers inside about some of the devastating effects of re-entering into society after a long prison term. For example, the new drug crack and its effects on families and communities is something that would be new for a guy that had been in jail before this type of drug came out. He might not understand how someone could rob his mother for crack.

Unfortunately, I was unable to make the right connections, and my parole officer told me [paraphrasing], "The first thing you do I am locking your black ass up." He insisted that I stop doing the volunteer work, show him a pink slip and replace it with a pay stub. I stopped working at the youth center on 110th St. and 5th Avenue in January 1989. That parole officer was on some stuff. I even called my mother and discussed him with her. My mother advised me to change parole officers by speaking with his supervisor. I thought about it, but I also thought about making enough money and just leaving the city and parole and saying f--k it.

I hustled around town until finally I got a job working for a temporary agency that was almost like a scam, doing construction work. I would normally have been paid about $12 an hour, but I only earned the minimum wage at the agency. One particular place I worked for liked the way I worked so much (i.e., like a machine) that they asked me to work for them permanently, as opposed to working for the agency. I accepted, and I started making $135 a week (net pay) for about 60 hrs. This was not enough to maintain myself, much less my daughter too. In fact it was like a joke because I had to pay $70 rent for a room, $12 for carfare back and forth to work, and I had to eat seven days a week. I had a phone installed in my room and I had to have clothes. With this pay and my expenses I could barely take care of myself, not to mention my child. I was constantly faced with the temptation to do better by selling drugs. So, I started to hustle a little on the side. Things were going well until I realized that my bosses were racist Jews. They owned a furniture warehouse where I loaded and unloaded tractor trailers every day and stacked things as they came in. There were several floors of all types of furniture. They had bars, dining room sets, living room sets, recliners, bedroom sets, etc. However, all these people seem to know was money, gain, and profit. They didn't care, and they were dogging me and the other brothers. They said things like, "Move it! Move it! Move it!" very fast as we were carrying couches or dressers on our backs. One day I told them, "You move it!" and I quit. They had hired me from the temporary agency and had given me two raises upon demand, but I didn't think $135 a week while working overtime was worth all the s--t I had to go through with them.

R$R

I decided that I could only get back on my feet by selling drugs. I began by taking what little money I had and bought some cocaine to cook up, since this seemed to be the fastest selling drug. I made a 100% profit, and I doubled up on the next package. I met this guy named Roger and asked him to get down with me. I just told him, "Look, I have four $25 bags of coke. You are down with me on all of this, but we have to build it up." He agreed and told me that we could sell in his old projects called the Washington Projects, between 2nd and 3rd Avenue. The problem was, we needed an approval or a certain color top to sell there. I knew people, so I went to someone (Chris from 100th Street) who had already made his bone up in the Washington Projects but was no longer selling there. It was sort of like going to one of the Dons in the *Godfather* to ask permission for turf. I didn't want any trouble, so I figured it was best to do it this way. Chris granted the permission for me to come out with the tops that he used to use, that were called The Tall Blues.

I went back to my partner Roger, who was young and didn't know that I was an old-timer with a little influence, myself. "Yo, we got the Tall Blues," I told him. "That is somebody else's tops," he said. "Don't worry about it. I took care of everything." I then called my daughter's uncle and suggested we get together. We got together, made a truce, and he became part of our little four-bag enterprise. He would take some of what we made and sell it in the Bronx. We bought the tall bottles and the sky blue tops, and the word spread that the Tall Blues was back out. Word also spread that Shaky was back, and he had it. Some people who were new around the way wanted to know who the hell was Shake.

As time went on, I had one guy who used to buy 20 bottles at a time from me. I asked him one time when he came to re-up, "Yo, what's your name?" "Robert," he said. "Yo, Robert, I like your style. Would you like to get down with us? You will be down as a partner with everything we have." He said, "Bet," and he put what he had together with what we had. Robert had just come home from doing about 12 years and things would begin to move.

We had a meeting like the regular gangsters do in the *Godfather*. At the meeting, it was decided that Robert would be the bill collector, Roger would be the pickup man, and I would pretty much be the person who kept s--t organized. It may seem like an easy task, but nothing is in the world of the underground. I began to accumulate all the bullets and shotgun shells I could because we started to make noise (i.e., make money). The first gun we got was a 32 from Universal Starchild (Too Tough's uncle). We then got hold of a sawed-off 12-gauge shotgun.

One day, Robert told a guy who sold in the same area as us for years that he could no longer sell there. In Robert's mind the guy was a coward, and, besides, it was time to get money, f--k that. We got to the point where we could let a crack head hold our product and pitch for us. One time, a guy stopped a customer who happened to be going by the building where we sold. Robert, Roger and me happened to be standing across from the area. Robert said, "Yo! Did you see that? F--k that s--t! We are not going to be having that." When the guy who had stopped the customer came whistling by us, Robert stopped him. "Yo, my man. What the f--k you doing f----g with our customers?" Robert asked him. The guy looked scared because when Robert said this Roger and I stepped right up, real serious-like, with Robert. Before the guy could answer, Bam! Robert slapped the piss out of money. I would learn that this was Robert's favorite past time. Immediately, the guy tried to flee, but I was on his right and Roger was on his left. I was in good shape (I had boxed upstate for years), so my hands were nice. Bam! Bang! I hit him with a two-piece left, and then a right. All of a sudden, Robert grabbed the guy and threw him into a fence where people walked their dogs, and Robert started kicking the s--t out of money. Robert later emphasized to me the need to draw blood. In fact, he later had his helpers collect bills and paid them only if they brought him blood on a handkerchief.

People were noticing what was going on, although I was just living from day to day. Money started coming in a little better, and we were able to spend. We bought a triple beam scale, a thing called a sealer, and other materials needed for expansion. We were able to get an apartment in the projects to work our drugs out of. Roger had an aunt named Tina who used to get high. We paid her in product and some cash for the use of her apartment. We kept the refrigerator full and crack head girls used to love to come there. They could get food, drugs, and some good d--k from time to time.

We started selling drugs 24 hours a day from inside and outside the apartment. We used to have customers searched with the sawed-off shotgun pointed at them. This way, word got around that if you wanted to stick Shake and them up, you better be right. We did not allow anyone to see the back room; this kept people in suspense.

One day my sister's little sister Puff came up to me and told me that she had a friend that could help me sell. I told her to take 20 bottles and give them to him and get back to me. The next day, Puff had all the money. "Where is your friend?" I asked her. She brought him to me; he could not have been more than 13 years old. He had been selling drugs for years and had mad clientele. He knew all the people who smoked in school. His name was Mike; he became a runner for us.

I cased our spot and told Robert and Roger that we needed to get walkie-talkies and make sure that we had escape routes. We went to Third Avenue and bought some nice walkie-talkies.

People started to bring us everything. We had a house full of TV's, radios, Walkman's, VCR's, and a bunch of other items, as if we were some kind of fences. People also brought us jewelry: we decided that Robert would get all the chains that came through, I would get all of the rings, and Roger would get the other things, like Cuban bracelets and s--t. I had a neck full of rings with different rubies and diamonds. Robert had mad chains on his neck, and Roger had all kinds of s--t. We tried to always break things down fairly between us when we split s--t.

Sometimes, since we had guys from the Bronx and Brooklyn down with us, I would have everybody meet up at the same time in the Washington Projects for a show of our strength. One time when we were all there, we saw somebody who owed some money come strutting by us. He became recreation. Somebody said, "Yo, there goes Sammy, that nigger that owes us some money." Everybody took off after him, and we caught him. It was a hot summer day in broad daylight. People watched from their windows and a woman said, "Leave that poor boy alone! You're going to kill him." But we were powerful and ruthless. "Shut the f--k up, old lady and mind your business," was the response she got.

We began riding in limousines just to hang out. I had a girl who I paid to pick up for me, cook up for me, and bottle up the drugs. All of this was happening too fast. I got a girlfriend because Samantha was a hopeless case. The girl I was messing with was named Cathy. Cathy was fresh out of a rehab center when I met her. It didn't take long before she was my girl, and everybody knew it.

Cathy held up for a little while, and I began to care for her a lot. One evening she came to me and told me that she had been smoking crack and had had some drinks. I told her that she should not do that. What else could I do? Another day she came and told me that she had sniffed some dope. I watched her fall off and that hurt me. One day, I got a bag of coke from my spot, got Cathy, and began sniffing in front of her, asking her if that was what she wanted, for me to start sniffing and we both go down. She laughed and said, "Nigger, give me some of that coke s--t." That was the beginning of my relapse.

Cathy became pregnant and lost the child because of the drug use. She then met up with one of her old boyfriends who had had her on the stroll and strung out. She was still sort of soft on the guy, and we fell off. I still saw her because she cared too much for me to just dump me.

One day, this guy came up to me named Charles who I had known for some time and asked me if I wanted to buy a Black and Decker drill. I bought the s--t for a bottle of crack. The next time I saw Charles, he asked me for some drugs to sell. He told me that he could sell them in Connecticut. I denied him the first time, but eventually gave him something to sell. That would be the worst mistake I ever made.

There we were, built up into a little empire. We stamped our drugs R (for Robert), $ (for Shaky), R (for Roger). Hence, R$R. One day, business was going well and Roger came to tell me he was ready to re-up. He had about $ 2,000 on him, and money and drugs at the spot. I told him to go get our re-up girl, Sylvia, and go straight to re-up, and I was going to go over to the spot, make a 30-second money pick up and get out of there. He said, "O.K." and left.

I left the spot (a lady named Bee Bee's house where we paid for the use of an apartment) and went to the spot in the Washington Projects. When I arrived, I found Roger had not done what we said he was going to do. Instead, he was in the house playing with the money and hanging out with the girls. Just the day before, I had held a meeting and told them all how important it was for them to stop bringing the girls up there and to realize that this was a spot, not a hang out. I went in and started pitching a b---h because things were not going as they should have been. A second later, there was a knock at the door and in my anger I said, "Who the f--k is it?" "Police!" was the response I got. Then it all hit me at once: *Oh, s--t! I am on 12 years parole. There are drugs, guns, shotguns, bullets, and all kinds of hot s--t in here.* I took the escape route I knew of, which was to climb down the four flights; I was out of there in two minutes flat. Seconds later, others came out of the window because they had panicked too. The wire that was used to get away on popped, and several people were left inside. One guy who we paid for security asked me to come over and catch him as he jumped from the fourth floor. He weighed 249 pounds, and I weighed 137 pounds. Hell no, I wasn't about to try that. He panicked and jumped. I heard the sound of wood crack as he shattered both his legs and his arm, and fractured his neck. Seconds later, dope, bullets, guns, etc. were coming out of the window. The others who were in the house were young and did what they felt was most important, which was to get rid of the drugs because the police sounded as if they were going to kick the door in at any time. They had also stacked about $2,000 inside the closet, wrapped in a sheet.

The spot was getting hot, so I left a person to keep me informed of what happened, and I went to Bee Bee's. Seconds later, I got word that the guy who was injured had told the police that he had come to buy and I threw him out the window. Now I really began to panic and decided I would have to lay low for a while. I went to the spot the next morning, got the $2,000, and went on the run. I figured that it was all Roger's fault anyway, so what the f--k.

Pimping Ain't Easy

I went downtown to a hotel on 86th St. and rented a room for a week. I had a little money left, although I had just lost everything else that was in the apartment that was busted. While downtown, I tried to cool out but I was getting bored and the excitement was calling me back uptown.

No one knew where I was. I needed some clothes, so I went uptown to the Douglas Projects, where my sister's sister's brother, Joey, lived. I used to stay with him, so I had clothes there. When I arrived, I was told that my parole officer had been looking for me. He had been flashing his gun and a photograph of me subtly. I grabbed a few things and left.

I figured I'd stop by the East River Projects and see my old girlfriend Cathy, when I ran into Debbie. Debbie was a lady who smoked crack and had f--ked my homeboy Robert. I told her that I was downtown and on the run. I explained to her what happened and that things were rough. She asked me if I had some coke, which I did. I told her to get some Phillie cigars and we'll get high.

We went on the roof of the East River Projects and got high together. She told me how hard her life had been, and how she'd learned to survive in the streets. Then, she surprised me with a proposition: she asked me to be her pimp. "What!" I said to myself, while casually telling her, "No problem. Pimp, I am." She told me that she'd take care of me. She explained to me that she was doing this because she wanted to, not because she had to. I asked her about Robert, and she said that there was nothing there. Women! She told me that she needed to get her get-up and that she would meet me at the hotel that night (that's when she usually worked).

I broke out and didn't really think much about it because I had been propositioned like this before. I had gone through a brief episode of this, which lasted for about three days and ended with me catching gonorrhea. I learned that the women we least suspect of whoring are truly whores already, but we just don't know it. They look like our mothers and aunts, dressed up and looking pretty.

Sure enough as the world revolves, the Debbie's arrive. She wore a pair of black pumps, a blue dress, a long black wig, some dark shades and some makeup. It was time for her to teach me some things about the night world of tricks, hookers, pimps, and simps. "Wait here," she told me, "and as I turn my trick I'll bring you the money. Oh yeah, we need a new name for you. Do you like the name Boss?" I said, "It sounds good to me." "Then, Boss Daddy it is," she said, and she left.

About 40 minutes later, she returned very hyper, handed me $50, and said, "Here is some reefer. This s--t is good. This white trick has a whole lot of this s--t. I'll be back. I have to go." And she left.

I sat there with $50 and a big ass bag of reefer. I rolled up a joint and thought to myself, *this is going to be all right*. Later, she returned with about $100. "Here baby," she said. "Can I have some coke since we have some money and I am going to work all night?" "Alright," I said. Who was I to say no? S--t, she made the money, I didn't. She was leaving to go buy some coke when she asked me if I wanted some Phillie cigars. I told her to get me some. She returned with a box full of cigars and some coke. She cooked it up, and I made some woolas (i.e., reefer and base coke mixed together in cigar paper). I began to like this get-high more and more, Debbie was turning me out. This scenario went on for a while, until one day Debbie started telling me how I should be, what I should do and or not do on the strip. She told me that a b---h is not supposed to say anything to me, and how to charge a woman who chooses me. How I should not walk on the side of the street where the hookers were. She explained that a blowjob went for $35, and a f--k for

$50; hence, half and half would be about $75. She explained to me that time-wise it was $100 an hour, so if a b---h left at 8:00 a.m. with a trick and came back twelve hours later at 8:00 p.m., she should have a total of at least $1,200. This is because she lets the trick know that this is the going rate for this piece. She also taught me about counting the condoms the whores had in their purse and how each one used would represent no less than $35 a blow job. Therefore, if a whore left with 10 condoms and came up $5 short of 35*10 ($350), then there was a problem that I would have to straighten out. "We have to get some other girls in the stable," she said. She told me that she I should try to get some other girls. I spoke with this girl named Denise, who was Puerto Rican, and she agreed to join up with us. When Denise arrived at the hotel, Debbie told her that I was her man and, she loved me very much, and Denise would have to treat me with just as much love as she did. She also told her that she would have to do like I tell her. She then told Denise, "Strip so Daddy and me can see what you got." Denise did what she was told. Then Debbie had Denise turn around and spread her cheeks. After a thorough examination, Debbie told Denise to shower. While Denise was in the shower, Debbie told me that she was going to the store and that I should f--k Denise if I wanted to. I did.

That night Denise got high for free while Debbie did all of the work. The next night Denise was supposed to go out and work. Denise claimed that she didn't like the hoe stroll and she had other people and places that she went to. So Debbie told her to go and to come home later on that night. When it was getting really late in the morning, Debbie and I wondered if Denise was going to show. Finally, she did.

Denise came in with her clothes torn a little bit and told us some cockamamie story about how she fell asleep and somebody robbed her and took her shoes. Debbie looked her over close and said, "Don't worry." Denise took that as meaning everything was cool. Denise then tried to get in the bed with us. Debbie told her, "B---h, don't ever try to get in the bed like that without taking a shower. Get in the shower first."

As Denise went into the shower, Debbie spoke to me, "Listen, I am going to go to the store. I want you to talk pimp talk to this hoe. Tell her that she is to do like you tell her," and then Debbie left.

Denise came out of the shower, still with this look of innocence on her face as if somebody had actually taken her shoes and money while she was asleep. "Come here Denise," I told her. She came over to me while I was lying on the bed. I slapped her, and she looked amazed. It wasn't a hard slap because I really didn't have that type of style in me. I then began to run off the lines that Debbie had given me: "Let me tell you one motherf----g thing, hoe," I continued. "You are my f----g hoe and you do what the f--k I tell you to do. Do you understand me?" "Yes daddy", she told me. I continued, "Don't ever come in here and tell me that f----g stupid s--t you told me tonight. Now get the f--k over here in the bed." Debbie returned and asked me if I had spoken with Denise. I told her that I had.

By that time, I had started to go back and forth uptown again, but I wasn't hustling anymore. Roger and Robert had started up the spot again, but I didn't get with that. One day, I met this tall, brown-skinned, green-eyed female. However, I knew she was a whore. Although I had never seen her before, I was starting to get to know a whore's walk, talk, and overall demeanor. For example, Debbie had the mean hoe stance, the way they stand when they are trying to pick up a trick. So there I was, uptown, trying to speak with this woman. I tried to throw the mean game on her, but it didn't work. I went upstairs to see Bee Bee, who was a "whoreologist." She had turned out more young pimps than anybody I knew. She used to tell stories about how one girl sat on this pimp's lap and the pimp looked at her and said, "B---h, do you know who I am? I'm a pimp and I charge b----es to sit on my lap." Bee Bee told the story of how the pimp charged this girl $1,000 for sitting on his lap, and she paid it. She told us about the pimps who she knew that made it big and bought Rolls Royce's.

As Bee Bee was telling one of her ancient stories, Debbie walked in, and on her right arm was the tall brown beauty I had just tried to get. Debbie asked me to step aside a minute and told me that this girl was going to become one of the family. I just smiled. I told Bee Bee that I was going to stay there that night, and the other girl went and took a shower. Debbie, the new girl (Candy), and me all climbed into the bed together. Here I was with two beautiful young women who were mine, butt-naked in the bed with me. I made love to them both.

I got some silk dresses from my sister for both Debbie and Candy. They would walk down the street with me, one on each arm. My sister had some expensive silk dresses and to see those two women dressed in silk walking with me was something for the people in the community. I later saw Cathy who told me that she had heard about my new game. She sounded almost jealous and told me that she used to make money at Hunts Point. I said to myself, *all that time I was giving you all that money and you was a hoe.* "So, what's up? You going to join the family, or what?" She told me that she would think about it.

After a while, I realized that there was a lot of money being made, but Debbie only wanted to get high. I tried to encourage her to stop getting high because we could have more money that way. This caused a problem. Candy proved to be an idiot. I would have to look for her all over the place. As for Denise, I chased her up and down the street, telling her that she violated by fronting on me. I asked her how in the hell was she going to sell me that damn dream about being down, and then just leave. I ended up hitting her with a pipe and almost breaking her leg. She went to this kid named Wally O and told him about me. I told Wally O, in front of her, that I have no problem with him having her, but the b---h was being charged. He could either pay the charge, or I would shake her down every time I saw her. So, that's what I did.

Denise would have money in her bra, in her shoe, in the cracks in between her toes, etc. Sometimes I used to let my lower desires get the best of me when I found out that she didn't have any money. I used to just tell her to perform. She would do a wonderful job of buffing me in a few minutes, without even getting on her knees.

There was one other girl who said that she would be down with this program but changed her mind. I would go to where she was and tax her for not fronting. She gave me a problem at first, but I had gotten tired of the crack head lies and I told her, "Stop playing yourself, b---h. Now you are being charged until I feel you have paid enough. Whenever I come to this door, I want you to hit me off with some loot, do you understand?" I poked her in the mouth with my index finger real hard and busted her lip. She went and got me some money, and it was clear that she understood.

The problem with all of these girls was that they were crack heads, and I had become a woola head. Eventually Debbie got tired of my trying to tell Denise to stop getting high and spending all the money. Denise was not trying to hear that type of reasoning. The last straw was when I went to speak with her one time and she tried to pull a trick. As I was calling her, she was giving me the chill sign because she was trying to rope this guy. I got upset and went over to the stroll side and slapped her into the next day. Then I told her to come here, like a Neanderthal man. She came and listened to me, and then she said, "Shaky, you should not have done that. I was trying to get the trick, and that is what it is about. I would have seen you later, but when I am out here I am trying to get the money. Besides, remember that I told you that I am doing this for you because I want to, not because I have to." I felt kind of stupid. I understood what she was saying.

Word got to me that my sister Elaine was on the stroll sometimes. I didn't believe this. One night as I came to check on one of my b---hes, who turned the corner but my sister? "Yo, what's up, babe? You choosing?" I asked her. I hadn't seen Elaine in a long time. She smiled and asked me what I was doing out there. I told her.

I wanted to get Elaine out of that life. I contacted her old boyfriend and asked him to try to speak with her. He came downtown and looked for her. Finally, he found her and told her that he would give her plane fare to Florida. That night my sister and I stayed together. Boy, was that night something. Let me tell you about it: Elaine and I stayed in a hotel in Harlem near the YMCA. Several days before that, I had robbed a man for about $3,000, and I had about $1,500 left on me. So, while we were in the hotel I decided to send Elaine off with a party, so to speak, and we began getting high together. Elaine smoked the pipe, and I smoked the reefer with base cocaine and Phillie cigar wrappers. Everything seemed all right for a while. I had never seen my sister get high off of freebase. All of a sudden, Elaine started to act strange. She started getting very paranoid. I had never seen a person act that way. She put her index finger to her mouth and motioned to me to be very quiet. Then she jumped to the floor and started crawling on the floor. I said to her, "Elaine what's wrong, baby?" She was starting to scare me very much. I had never seen that done before; those who smoked woola didn't react that way. It was almost like the difference between mild retardation and profound retardation. The next thing I knew, Elaine started to look on the floor for s--t. I figured she wanted to have some more coke, so I went to buy her some more. When I returned to the hotel, she opened the door and motioned to me with her index finger again to be quiet. She did this all night. She kept her ear near the base of the door as if someone were there. I kept saying, "Elaine, there is no one there." I can now see how people commit murder and get murdered because of crack. My own sister was scaring the s--t out of me. If I had had a gun at the time, I would certainly have cocked it and kept it on standby.

The next morning we got together with her ex-boyfriend, and we saw her off to Florida. She has been there ever since. I watched as her plane pulled off and I wondered should I have gotten on that flight as well.

Debbie ended up leaving. She was on Columbus Avenue and other hoe strolls with the other b---hes that had run off. I found myself like a jack rabbit, jumping from hole to hole looking for them. I wasn't working and things got so bad that I robbed people to stay alive. I was on the run; my girls had left me. Debbie didn't tell me the part about always being independent in case your whores leave; I learned this the hard way.

I ate at schools or wherever free breakfast and lunch were given out. There were two people who would do what they could, though: my sister's little sister Puff, and her grandmother. They would not see me go hungry, no matter what. It is understandable that some people could be so disappointed with their loved ones or friends that they simple turn off rather than on to them.

I couldn't maintain the rent at the hotel with no money from the girls, so I went uptown. I tried to stay with Cathy, and from time to time she would let me. Sometimes, because of pride, I refused to go into a shelter or to beg someone for a resting place for the night. As a result, I even slept in the hallways sometimes or up on the roof of some building. I went to a hotel or a fire hydrant to maintain my hygiene, at least. I was at a very low point in my life. I have to say that my life was unmanageable. I don't think I knew where I was really headed, and I felt I had lost all of the knowledge that I had ever gained. I just wanted things to fall into place for me. I wished that a million dollars would just appear and the parole would end. Despite everything, I felt that there was some hope; I felt something would break sooner or later. I had forgotten my idea of forming an organization called RAW. The goals that I had thought of while in prison were shattered by the raw realities around me; things were rough. I was on parole and on the run. I was homeless, lost, and unstable. This is not what I had planned.

Now that I think about it, everyone that I hung out with was an addict (except DeeBo), even my so-called friends. Every one of the females was an addict, which probably no doubt led to their prostitution. Charles, Girl Cathy, Baby Doll, Debbie, Denise, Candy, even my sister Elaine, were all sick! There is little help one who is an addict can get from another addict, unless one of them is recovering.

I was at a very low point. At times, I wish I had made contact with my man uptown who said he was going to help me. Another old friend named Popeye told me that he was going to give me something on July 28, 1989: a whole bag full of crack. He was going to re-up, and he was going to give me all of the crack that his workers had left over. He was going to give it to me for free; this was supposed to help me get on my feet. I believed him because he had looked out for me before. He knew me and he knew my potential. He had watched it for the quick run I had.

The morning of July 28 I got up and went to fix a slow leak I had in a tire of my ten-speed bike. After fixing it, I was going to go uptown to see my man who had usually looked out for me. This was the person who had given me the 50 quarters of dope years ago. He had told me to hold on because he was going to hit me soon.

I was on my way uptown on the bike when I ran into somebody who owed me a few dollars, but had been ducking me for a couple of months. His name was Charles and he was with a bad b--ch named Baby Doll. She had given me a blow job one time that was out of this world. She had swallowed my jism with a smile and had then said, "That was good." She hadn't spilled a drop, nor had I paid a dime. She liked me.

I really needed the money at that time. So I called to him, "Yo, Charles, where is the money you owe me?" He replied, "I don't have it." "What?" I asked, "What the f--k you mean you don't have it?" As I spoke, I motioned to get off the bike to try to scare him, or keep him honest. At that second, Charles ran across the street. I went over and asked Baby Doll if Charles had money on him. She said that he had spent $6 on some crack and he was showing her where he had been, but that he didn't have any money. She then asked me, "But why did he run like that, Shake?" "Because he has been lying to me for a while now," I told her.

About two minutes later, Charles arrived in a police car and pointed me out for having allegedly robbed him. The police asked me not to move, and they searched me. They found the tools I had used to fix the flat: six patches, a butter knife, a pair of pliers, a whistle on a red string, some glue, and 60 cents. That was all I had. I tried to explain to them that I knew Charles and that he owed me some money. I was very nervous because I knew that I was on the run and once they ran my fingerprints I would be in trouble. However, they had a crack head psychopath who was scared half to death. I realize now what beating guys up in the community did, it made people scared of you. They handcuffed me and took me in for questioning.

There I was, in a police car on the way to the precinct for a robbery that never happened. After being in society for a few months, I found myself in police custody. I wanted to get out of there so bad. I couldn't believe what was happening. "What's your name?" they asked me. "Eugene Serrando," I told them. I figured that if I stalled for time I could get them to get Baby Doll, who would confirm the truth about what happened. She could also confirm that Charles had no money and that he was never robbed, because she was right there. The police asked me what happened, but they changed the story around to fit their needs, which was to get a conviction if possible. They had a crack head, some tools they could make a crime with, and an ex-con who had just served time in prison for robbery. If nothing else, they were going to try the case. The only problem was how.

The Perfect Lynching

The six months run was over; I was going through the system again. I could feel it, smell it, and sense it all over again. First, I went through central booking, then to the Manhattan detention center for men. Before I knew it, I was about to be arraigned. A parole warrant had been dropped, and I was notified within 48 hours that they were aware of my location and re-arrest. These people worked fast and efficiently when it was to their advantage. It's sickening they way they behave when you need something from them that doesn't imply anything in it for them.

There I was, sitting in the bullpen (where detained prisoners wait before going in to see the judge). The district attorney called my name: "Eugene Serrando." I should have noticed the sell-out coming, but I didn't because I was ignorant to the pitfalls, tricks, and traps set within the system (i.e., deals worked out between the defense attorneys and the district attorneys). "Yeah! Right here!" I exclaimed, as I went willingly to the chopping block. I walked over to the gate, which had bars on the cage. Those bars were the only things separating me from the district attorney. I guess some guys who knew the system better had assaulted some of those phony bloodsuckers.

My attorney began by saying, "Good morning, Mr. Serrando. My name is Mr. Locker and I have been assigned to handle your case." I listened to him very attentively as he continued, "Where were you May 5th?" I answered, "I don't remember right off hand, that was two months ago." He responded, "Well, the complainant says that you and seven other guys beat him up and took $2." "What?" I was going crazy with what I had just heard. I couldn't believe that I was hearing this correctly. Where the hell did this bulls--t come from? Locker kept going and paid no attention to my cues. He only wanted to allow me to calm down long enough for him to continue. After all, this was an everyday thing that he was used to going through. Besides, he wasn't getting much money from this case like the J.J. Gotti case that was being held in the same court during the same time period. "Where were you on June 15th?" he asked. I told him I didn't recall off hand. He came back with the same rehearsed story, "Well, the complainant says that you and seven guys beat him up and took $2." "What the f--k is this s--t?" I asked. Locker paused again: cool, calm and collected as he savored all this and enjoyed watching a plan come together. Finally he responded without remorse, "You're being charged with three robberies. The district attorney is offering you six to life." I listened as I tried to get my thoughts together. I responded faintly, without really being cognizant, "But I am innocent." His voice brought me back to reality, "It doesn't look good. They have a complainant, you have a record. How old are you now? 29? You'll be 35 when you get parole if you go to trial and blow. Well... you'll be doing a lot of time." The fix was in and I later learned that it was simple statistics. If I have a bag with three green balls and one red ball, and if I stick my hand in the bag to get a ball I have a 3 out of 4 chance of getting a green ball. Well, they fabricated three alleged robberies in the hopes of getting three, two, or one conviction. The chances were greater that way. The district attorney was a young pissed-colored nigger who was slick and ambitious for the cause of the destruction of his own people. He was black, whether he realized it or not.

I spoke to Locker as sincerely as I could, "I don't want one day because I didn't rob Charles. I know him. He is lying." "Alright," he said, "we'll be seeing the judge in a little while," and he left to go report to his homeboys, the district attorney, and the judge with whom he probably played backgammon. This s--t was all about the continued destruction of the black man by any means necessary (i.e., imprisonment, drug distribution, mis-education, white institutionalized racism, etc.).

After being in society for a few months I found myself incarcerated and facing 37 1/2 years minimum to 86 years maximum for a crime that was never, ever, f----g committed! Was I angry? Am I still angry as I write this? Excuse my language, but I deliberately left it as such as an indicator of my anger. More specifically, yes, I am very hurt and angry. Anyway, it was at that moment that I realized how strong the system was and how much slavery was still in effect. It was just as easy in 1989 to snatch a black man off the street, chain him up, lock him down, and convict him of some bulls--t so he would be a slave once again.

Preliminary Trial

At the preliminary hearings, damn near everything my attorney requested was denied. Many papers (written statements of the witness' interview) turned up missing that could have helped prove my innocence and exonerate me. It was brought out that the complainant had an extensive history of psychiatric evaluations, but the defense was denied access to the records because proving a man's innocence was not as important as getting a guilty verdict. My attorney put in what I later learned is called an "omnibus motion." In this motion, he explained to the court the following:

"That it is apparent that neither the defendant nor counsel has sufficient information to prepare a complete and adequate defense unless the allegations contained in the indictment are amplified by the proper responses to the bill of particulars and the discovery annexed hereto. The information requested is necessary for the proper preparation of the case and effective representation of the defendant at trial."

In number three of my attorney's discovery, the following documents were requested:

From Supporting Affirmation
Indictment #8562/89

3) Provide copies of any and all reports, papers, forms or memorandums of the N.Y.P.D., any other law enforcement agency or other government agency relating to the above entitled case, or any part thereof; including but not limited to: Form UF61, DD5, DD9, 911 tapes, sprint run and form, arrest reports, booking reports, volcher alarms, radio transmissions, command advisories and all other papers and documents

concerning the investigation of the alleged crime/s and
the arrest of defendant.

I was denied many of the above. Defense did not in fact get the
amplification of the bill of particulars. For example, Locker requested in
his motion that any and all material, whether written statements or
otherwise, be turned over to the defense, especially such material which
may have been given to any law enforcement agency and which is
exculpatory in nature. I had always thought that this law (i.e., Rosario
Material) would protect the innocent in the interest of justice. How does
the system get away with blatantly railroading guys like that?   Is it
because nobody really seems to give a damn? The powers that be have
no real checks and balances because those who are supposed to check
and balance the system are too engrossed in the system.

Violation of Due Process:
Rosario Material

From the outset, this case entailed the word of the complainant against the defendant. There was another eyewitness who gave a sworn affidavit stating that she in fact did know the defendant to be innocent in that she was there with the complainant when the alleged robbery had taken place.

Allegedly, there was a 911 call made to the police precinct by the complainant from his home that the police were supposed to have responded to (some five years later, the actual 911 recording was still being requested by the defendant). These recorded statements were requested in the omnibus motion by the original trial lawyer well within the time for the district attorney to have them turned over. Any law enforcement agency is a branch or arm of the district attorney; hence, any negligence on its part is the responsibility of the district attorney. So, the fact that these statements were requested and not turned over was the district attorney's fault. These statements were especially important for two major reasons: firstly, this was a case involving a crack addict with psychiatric history; secondly, the case involved that same addict's word against the defendant. Where any statements made by the complainant pertaining to the case are relevant, and, at minimum, in the interest of justice, the defense should have the opportunity to scrutinize them prior to or during trial where they are relevant. If there was no call, then there was a lie from the outset. This is what I believe may have taken place: If there was a call, it is believed that the complainant may have said something like, "This guy is bothering me." The retriever of the call may have asked "Are you, or have you been hurt?" The answer: "No!" "Did he rob you?" The answer again: "No!" There was no way of knowing the particulars since the statements were withheld. If those statements had been exculpatory, as the defendant believes they may have been, then the case would never have advanced beyond the grand jury and received the indictment.   This was a trick that the district attorney and the police both knew and I had to learn about the hard way.

After the alleged call, the complainant went to the precinct and an officer named Robert Furman (who turned sergeant during or shortly after my conviction) conducted an interview with him.   During this interview, a lot of things were said to the interviewing officer. In fact, the officer made a call to the complainant's home to verify who he was. I could hear the conversation: "Do you have a son named Charles Wilder?" Response: "Why?" "Because he has a man here under some serious charges and he has told me over a hundred stories already. That's why!" Bam! End of conversation. This same officer interviewed me and was given statements about what happened. I told him that there was an eyewitness who could tell them that I did not rob this guy and that this guy, in fact, owed me $25.

Later, this officer lost all of the original written reports of the interviews conducted with the complainant and with me. When he came to court, he had what he called a formal report, which is a typed report. He claimed that he had not changed anything in the formal report that had been in the written report.   The district attorney, realizing the violation, immediately told the judge that he knew nothing about any written report.   When he was asked whether or not he added or left anything out of the formal reports allegedly given by the complainant, he said that he couldn't remember. My attorney moved for a mistrial, but it was not granted. I told Locker to try to subpoena get the statements that had the policeman on the phone telling the complainant's people that over 100 stories had been told subpoenaed from the phone company. Locker never was able to get the statements.

Pressure from the D.A.

and a Deal

The district attorney said that the complainant was being called and threatened everyday by me, despite the fact that I didn't even have the complainant's phone number. The district attorney then claimed to have had to move the complainant because I had had some guys go by the complainant's house and hit him in the head with a machete, for which he had to have six stitches.

This was a tactic used by the district attorney; the real reason was that some witnesses for the defense were going to be late coming in and my attorney had asked for a postponement. The judge would not grant the postponement, and in fact said that he wanted to "end this case within the next 24 hours" [paraphrasing]. I guess this was because of the J.J. Gotti case, where there were sections with signs that read "Press Only" all over Part 39. This forced me to take the stand before my witnesses did, whereas the normal procedure was to allow all the defense witnesses to be heard first. That way the defendant could better decide if he should take the stand. I was not rehearsed in the least. I was simply told that neither any previous statements nor my past record was going to be used. It was later found out after the trial and conviction that the complainant was never hit with any machete, and therefore no one went to him on some order from me. The same way he was never hit with any machete is the same way he was never robbed, but the courts expected me to believe that they could not use deductive reasoning.

DeeBo, Teddy, Puff, and other friends from around the way who knew that Charles was lying tried to speak with Charles about telling the truth. One time Charles told them that he was trying to drop the charges, but the district attorney was on vacation, and another time he told them that the district attorney would not allow him to drop the charges, that the district attorney told him not to discuss the case and that he didn't want to see another black man go to jail. The complainant also told the probation officer that he was trying to help me with my drug addiction. Wow. Thanks a lot, Charles.

I personally feel sad for Charles because I understand what he had gone through and that he was a victim just like me. However, not everyone felt this way. One of my friends said to me, "Yo, Shake! Let me leave him in the building with a pipe in his mouth and two in his f----g head. That stupid nigger is gonna get you a lot of time." "No!" I told my homeboy. "They are already lying on me, and that's all they'll need to say that I am ordering hits from the jail." "O.K." my homeboy told me and that was the last he wanted to say about it. He was serious and there is no doubt in my mind that he would have taken care of business. The trial was already rigged to make me look like some sort of extortionist, and they mentioned things like, "Don't you know Poppo? Isn't it true that your stepbrother just beat a murder trial in this courtroom and that these are known drug dealers?" After my lawyer allowed the district attorney to parade these statements before the jury my lawyer said, sipping on his coffee real relaxed-like: "objection" The judge then, realizing his cue, said: "Sustained. The jury will disregard the statements." How do you disregard such statements as: "He was in jail for six years. He just came home for committing crimes where he placed his interest above that of society." These statements were way out of the realm of the Sandovol ruling made at the sidebar and, what's more, they were prejudicial to the defendant and therefore rendered the trial unfair.

Charles came to trial with what appeared as a thrift shop suit that I figured the district attorney bought him, and a haircut paid for by the district attorney as well. He had been well rehearsed by the district attorney and I would certainly have given him an Academy Award for his performance because he put on a beautiful act. When the district attorney called his witness, I couldn't believe that Charles had come to court. Why was he doing this? I figured it out later. *Hmm,* I said to myself, *this is only an example of the effects of slavery and the magnitude to which we as a people are still caught up in and suffering from it.* Brainwashed indoctrination, fear of the system and its power, conformity and, simply put, being lost like a ship without a sail, or a voyager without a destination.

He took the stand, and you can imagine my face at this time. Charles told the jury that he did not know my family or me. He said he knew only of me. He lied. The fact is that we had worked together as president and vice president of a youth council, right there in our projects. His sister was the girlfriend of my sister's sister's brother. Charles tried to say that he didn't know either my sister or any of my brothers. We had lived in the same project for fourteen years; in fact, he had been to my house on numerous occasions. He told the jury that he did not smoke crack and that he hadn't seen me for six years because I was in jail. Hence, he corroborated the fabricated stories that he, the police, and the district attorney had all concocted together.

Prejudiced

When I received my trial minutes, I learned of the following conversation that took place at the judge's bench. The following are the characters:

Williams: the District Attorney
Locker: the Defense Attorney
(Charles) Wilder: the Complainant
The Court: the Judge

Williams: Sir, you told us earlier, you indicated that you didn't believe Mr. Serrando lived in your complex anymore. Why did you believe that?
Wilder: Because he had been in jail for a while.
Williams: No! No! No!
Wilder: All right, I believed he was. I don't know.
Williams: No, Mr. Wilder, what I'm asking is what had you believed about him and his family?
Wilder: I had understood they were thrown out, they were evicted.
Locker: Objection.
The Court: Come to the sidebar, please.

(At the sidebar, outside the hearing of the witness and the jury):

The Court: Did you anticipate that last answer?
Williams: No, no, no! Mr. Locker had asked him...
The Court: I know what he asked him.

Williams: All I wanted to ask, if he had been thrown out and had been evicted from the complex, based on his information. That's all.

The Court: The objection to the question is sustained. The answer will be stricken.

The above is page 111 of the trial transcripts. It is unclear to me how the above line of questioning has anything to do with the alleged robbery, especially since my family had not been living in that project since 1983, a total of at least 5 years. In addition, my family was not on trial for any robbery. They were all in Florida minding their own business. The sidebar discussion continued:

Locker: Well, it could go with respect to the other answer. I move at this time for a mistrial. Clearly I had not in any way opened the door, I had not opened the door to a question which would elicit such an answer.

The Court: Even though that was the answer, you had to admit that Mr. Williams didn't expect that. It wasn't what he was asking.

Locker: That's not the point. The witness is under the control of Mr. Williams. It's clear to me he did not admonish him sufficiently in terms of not saying anything about his past criminal record.

Williams: Well, Judge, you must remember, in terms of the question I was asking, Mr. Locker went through at least two or three questions on his cross about why didn't Carroll Wilder take them to the building, okay? And why didn't he volunteer that information, and the only thing…

The Court: Mr. Williams…

Williams: …the only thing I wanted to ask was that fact that, to his knowledge…

The Court: Mr. Williams, I don't doubt the relevancy. The problem is that the first answer okay, the first answer, the one you didn't expect, is prejudicial and to deal with it in the second answer is also perhaps more prejudicial than it is probative.

Williams: How would I handle the fact that Mr. Locker has tried to establish that Carroll Wilder could have taken...

The Court: It was already an encapsulated subject. You had a statement that he didn't take the police, and the response was okay, which Mr. Locker didn't expect, because I didn't believe that these people lived there anymore, okay? And that ordinarily...

Locker: Excuse me...

The Court: And what you would have found in cross-examination is the question, well isn't it true that you never told the police that you knew where the guy lived? And the People's redirect, well, they explained to us-- the question, why didn't you tell the police and the answer would be, because I knew he didn't live there. What happened was that all came out on the cross, and you're going a step further, and that step further is irrelevant. AND WHAT IS MORE, IT'S PREJUDICIAL.

Williams: Okay, Judge.

The Court: I don't know that the step further, the last answer, is sufficiently prejudicial to declare a mistrial. The first answer that Mr. Locker is now belatedly objecting to is a different matter.

Locker: There was a reason I let it stay that way. I thought it best not to object because of the nature of the question.

Williams: I have one more question

The Court: Your last question?

Williams: Are you looking for employment?

The Court: Well, I have to deal with the objection now. Would you give me a moment, and I'll tell you how I'm going to deal with it.

(The Court and his law assistant confer off the record):

The Court: I'm going to reserve on the motion for mistrial as to the first answer; that is that the defendant, I believe the defendant being in jail, I will strike both answers and tell the jury to disregard the answers, and tell them that obviously neither of those facts have anything whatsoever to do with the question of guilt or innocence in this particular trial, and then I'll cover it also later on in the charge, assuming I don't later grant the motion for mistrial.

Fish on Dry Land

I took the stand more out of emotion than anything else. I had never been to trial before or taken the stand. In an effort to defend myself, I fought desperately for my life. What I is indescribable. I told them how I had worked, how I had known Charles, how he borrowed money from me, how he was not "all there", and how I was innocent. I was ridiculed on the stand, and the judge allowed the district attorney to have a field day with me while my attorney sipped coffee. I would later read a story about Emmett Till where the same thing was done at the trial of his killers (i.e., they drank soda pops and made things look relaxed as opposed to a serious trial).

The trial was short. It was only Charles' word against mine. He was an addict who professed, in part, to being an addict, and I was the one that the whole court seemed to be after. Both the defense and the district attorney rested their cases. I was sent back to the bullpen to await the verdict.

I returned to the courtroom later for the verdict. The judge asked the jury, "How do you find the defendant?" "We, the jury, find the defendant guilty of..." I looked over at the jury, and I must confess that I wanted to shoot them all despite the fact that I had never shot anyone in my life. I didn't even hear them saying "not guilty" for two of the three cases. They had found me guilty of the alleged July 28th robbery while on my bike on the way uptown. I was acquitted of the May 5th and July 15th cases (with the imaginary seven guys). The district attorney was happy with this because he had made a victory from nothing. He was a new and upcoming district attorney, young and learning how everything worked. I know the feeling of seeing your potential being manifested; the problem is that sometimes we exercise our potential in the wrong way.

Before sentencing I went to see a probation officer, which is standard procedure. He was black also. I had been lied on by a black man, convicted by a black district attorney, and now I was meeting with a black probation officer. All black men can't be brainwashed, can they? Well, sad to say that the reality is that most of us are and this is one of the reasons reparations is a must.

The probation officer asked me what happened. I told him the truth, and it brought tears to my eyes as I did. I poured my heart out to this guy. I don't know why I was so naive and open hearted. He filed a report for the judge to review before he sentenced me. The report read as follows: I was a psychopath, maladaptive, antisocial, and I had no remorse. How do you have remorse for something that never happened? Not to mention that this country and government doesn't even have remorse for what they know for sure happened to the millions of black people who suffered and still suffer from slavery.

The judge half looked at me and asked me if I had anything to say before he sentenced me. I was too traumatized to say much of anything, but I said, "Your being on the bench for 19 years, I am sure you know that there is more than reasonable doubt in this case." I was also a little incoherent, but I told him that I was innocent. The judge said to me "It was the jury. The system is not perfect, but it's the only system we've got." This was the first time I had heard this bulls--t, though it may have some validity and it definitely sounded real slick, as we say in the subculture.

I was sentenced to 7 to 14 years as punishment for a robbery that never happened. The judge also recommended that I do only the minimum. I always tell people I was innocent and how the system railroaded me. However, most people say to me, "Oh boy, sure you were innocent, that's what they all say."

The primary issue is whether or not my case was prejudiced by the loss of the notes (i.e., the written statements of the complainant to the police officer). It is strange that these notes happened to disappear. It is even stranger that I had to be persistent about these notes. I can only imagine what could have happened if I had not been there while the notes were being written, or if I had not been persistent. My attorney acted as if he did not wish to inquire about the notes, despite my constantly telling him about them. The last and final thing that is strange about the missing notes is that they weren't even mentioned in the appeal. These notes were the most essential in that they would have exonerated the defendant. Even the statements that were allegedly recorded on the 911 tapes have never been turned over. Was there ever a call? If not, could we say then that there was never any probable cause in that the whole case begins around the alleged phone call that was supposed to have been made by the complainant?

Moreover, the defendant's request for a full disclosure of the complainant's voluntary admission into a psychiatric hospital for treatment of depression was denied. It is clear that the defendant didn't have the right to adequately confront his accuser and that the defendant was prejudiced against. The overall lies, framing, fabrication, and the disappearance of the notes should lead the reader to understand that we do not all get due process or fair trials. This trial was rigged from the outset. What is most dangerous about all of this is that the society in which we live in can be dangerous. Any time a person can be picked up on the street because of an alleged robbery and spirited away to a precinct, then run through the system and end up convicted and sentenced to serve 7 to14 years for a crime that never happened, it's sad. It felt like nothing had changed from the time when they used to pick my ancestors up, spirit them away, and put them into involuntary servitude. What is the difference?

I have included some of the trial transcripts so that one can see what actually took place. As I sat in prison during my last two years of the sentence, hoping to see daylight, I was afraid of society. I was afraid of the possibility of ending up in there again for a crime that never occurred. What was worse is that they were trying to pass a law that stated: three violent felonies and you are in for life. I already had two, so another mistake would have rendered me, for all practical purposes, dead!

Innocently Doing Time

I went back to the Manhattan house after sentencing, and my world began to cave in on me. I didn't want to be bothered or consoled. I cried like a baby in the open amongst the hardened criminals. The words "7 to 14 years for nothing" kept ringing and ringing in my mind, like eternity. I called W.B.L.S. radio station, tried reaching Oprah Winfrey, etc. for help. Nothing happened, and I couldn't get a number for Oprah at the time. Hi, Oprah!

Eventually, I got into a workout program. I worked as a porter and participated in a program that did skits for the population. I had about three visits while in the city jail. Before long, the familiar red and tan bus came to pick me up for Downstate. I was a state prisoner again, only this time I was innocent.

I stayed in Downstate briefly and was sent to Comstock Main for reception. Comstock held me for about six months. I went to religious services every Sunday just to get out of the cell because we were locked in 23 hours a day. While at the services, I'd raise my hand as the preacher spoke. Eventually, he would acknowledge my hand. I'd stand up and say, "Reverend, I understand Jesus loves me, but I need a lawyer. Can you help me?" He'd tell me that he would speak with me after the services. After the services he would offer to pray for me. I asked this question to practically every preacher or Muslim Imam I came across. Eventually, I became tired of the same old story, "I'll pray for you. Take it to the Lord in prayer." I even wrote to a bunch of churches in the street. I received two responses; they both said that they would pray for me. After all the prayers, I was still fighting to get out. Nonetheless, I appreciated those who truly prayed for me because I believed in prayer, even though I had not seen my prayers answered in this matter.

After the Comstock reception, I was shipped to Clinton main facility in Dannemora, New York. I didn't stay there long because I was shipped to the annex across the street. While in the annex I had a hard start. I was very bitter. Sometimes an officer would say, "Good morning, Mr. Serrando. How are you?" I would say, "You don't have to say good morning to me. I'm innocent, I don't belong here, and there's nothing good about being locked up innocently. Furthermore, you don't care about how I am doing because if I asked you to help me get a lawyer to get out, you would look at me crazy." I would then ask him, "Please don't speak to me anymore or say good morning to me."

I got a porter job, so I didn't have to have dialogue with the officers. I just did my job and that was it. I was then told to take a violence and drug program. I asked them why I needed to take these programs when I'm innocent. I was informed that I would need these programs in order to participate in the trailer visits and to possibly make parole. Caught in a catch-22 situation, I joined the Network Program, which consisted of drug and violence counseling. I signed up for college and did pretty well. I then took up a political position as a prisoner representative. I began to organize brothers to get involved with a black studies program to learn about their history, resulting in the administration locking me up and giving me 30 days keep-locked (i.e., solitary confinement).

It was at this time that I met Ms. Dorothy Williams, who was the fiancée of a brother named Kenny. Every time someone would go to the phone to call someone, I would go over there and say, "Yo, man. I need somebody to speak to. I have hardly any family and none in the city, so I am lonely." The brothers would look at me and laugh because they thought I was just joking. How would they know my family situation? They would say things like, "Yo, go ahead Justice, man. Stop lying." "I'm serious," I would tell them, but they wouldn't believe me.

Finally, one day this pleading paid off and somebody gave me a chance to speak with someone. Kenny said to me, "These guys are insecure, but I'm going to let you speak with somebody." I waited until I saw Kenny going to the phone, just in case he forgot. I was there before he dialed the number. He looked over at me and my eyes told him what time it was, but just to make sure I said, "Yo, Kenny. Let me talk to somebody, homeboy. I don't care if she is black, fat, a crack head, wino, or nothing. If your uncle is there let me speak with him because I am innocent, I don't belong here, and it is hard doing time like this. I am very stressed." He put me on the phone with his fiancée Dorothy. There I was, finally, on the phone and speechless. He said, "Talk!" "Hello," I said. She responded, "Hello." I was happy to hear a lady's voice because it had been a while. "Ask her does she have any friends," Kenny prodded me. I followed his instructions. "Kenny told me to ask you do you have any friends?" "No," she said. I told Kenny she said no. Kenny then told me to ask her if I could write her sister. I asked her and she agreed. I gave Kenny the phone back and I immediately began my letter.

Her sister's name was Bertha and I wrote her my honest thoughts and feelings. I had been praying for God to send me someone for some time. I had a chance to speak with her once on the phone for a brief few minutes. After that, I was in solitary confinement for thirty days. I was shipped back to the main facility, which was a maximum A prison. Later, I was released from solitary confinement. One day while in the yard, I was called for a visit. I hadn't had a visit in years and I told the officer that there obviously was some mistake in their calling me for a visit. I explained to him that I had been called for a visit before and some Spanish people were there for someone else. After arguing with the policeman, I went to the visit, not having any idea who had come to see me. I didn't even have anything decent to wear other than the state clothing because my family didn't send much. My mother would allow me two phone calls per month because she was having a hard time managing everything by herself. Who was she going to turn to for help with her bills? No, I couldn't push up on her too much for anything.

I had not received any pictures from Bertha, and I had only spoken with her once because I had been in keep-locked. I arrived in the visit room and asked the officer who was there and where was my visit. He motioned to the table where she was. This was all very exciting. I walked over to her anxiously, I was so happy she had come. Basically, I just said hello to break the ice. She was very humble-looking, she was sweet and pretty, most of all she seemed honest to me. I had never met any woman as honest as she appeared to be to me. I spoke with her and tried to be as honest as I could. I told her that we could be together forever from that day on.

Bertha

Bertha had four children by four different men. It didn't matter to me though. She tried to tell me how I didn't have to worry about her children because she would take care of her own responsibilities. She had so much pride, but I didn't like the idea of her not realizing that I was not that type of man. I explained to her how important family was to me, mainly because I always wanted to have more family. I explained to her that her children would be a part of me as she was. I asked her if she had any pictures of them. She had two pictures with her of the two littlest ones. Her children's names were Clinton, Natasha, Cicely, and Monique. Their ages ranged from 7 to 16 years old. Bertha sacrificed them a little to include me in her life. For some reason, she saw something in me. She helped me to believe in myself more, too. This was clear to me from her coming to see me all the way in Dannemora, which was 12 hours away from Brooklyn where she lived.

The more I saw Bertha, the more I began to love her and see her true beauty. I told her as much. I'll never forget the moment she told me she loved me, and the first time she asked me to kiss her. I knew then that I had to marry her, so I asked her. I explained to her that I wanted to express certain things to her that I could do only by making love physically, but this would only be possible if we were married. I felt at times that she was like a flower needing to be watered otherwise she would whither and die. She was the earth, and I was the one needed to provide the water. It was becoming frustrating for me because this woman was all I ever wanted and needed in my life. I wondered if she was actually heaven-sent, as I had prayed so many nights for God to send me someone like her. I told her about this and she just sat there and listened attentively.

In 1991 Bertha agreed to marry me after only a few months together. We were making plans to get married in Dannemora (my divorce had just gone through). However, again I was moved. This time I was sent to Green Haven Correctional Facility.

I immediately signed up for college. I applied for a black studies program, and I also attempted to improve my Spanish. By then I had learned to read, write, speak and understand a lot of Spanish. However, I felt the need to improve my Spanish some more. I was told that the Spanish classes were for the Spanish-speaking inmates only. I put in a grievance, which I lost, and then appealed and lost. I felt this was something that was discriminatory. In my mind, I saw it as another way to keep blacks from uniting and/or getting ahead. Many jobs in this country require that one be bilingual. My ancestors have fought and died here in this country, they have built this country on their backs for free labor, so my family and I should be trained to qualify for whatever jobs that are made available in this country. To deny us this right is wrong, even if one is in jail.

A double wedding took place on March 25, 1992; both Kenny and I married the two Williams sisters. On that day my wife informed me that her sister's boyfriend tried to rape her. This had me very upset; I called and spoke with the sister about it. Nothing really happened except that I don't think that he tried that again.

Bertha and I had a trailer visit several months later. She became pregnant our first time together. Unfortunately, she had a miscarriage, which I know hurt her deeply. Shortly after our trailer visit I put in a petition to the courts for Too Tough. This petition brought me to the city jail, Rikers Island, because I had to leave from there to go back and forth to the Bronx family court. The petition was to establish my parental rights. The child welfare agency wanted to terminate my rights; however, the judge ruled against this, ordered that the agency work with me, and that I file a paternity petition, which I did (*figure 1*).

Secs. 522, 523 F.C.A.   Form 5-1 (Paternity) 11-85

FAMILY COURT OF THE STATE OF NEW YORK
COUNTY OF **BRONX**

```
┌─────────────────────────────────────────┐
│              In the Matter of a           │
│            Paternity Proceeding.          │
│  MR. GRAYLING EUGENE FERRAND              │
│                           Petitioner,     │
│               — against —                 │
│  VALERIE LOOMIS                           │
│  775 CONCOURSE VILLAGE #17C               │
│  BRONX, NEW YORK  10451                   │
│                   ADDRESS   Respondent.   │
└─────────────────────────────────────────┘
```

Docket No.

PATERNITY PETITION
(Parent)

TO THE FAMILY COURT:

The undersigned Petitioner respectfully shows that:

1. Petitioner resides at G.C.FACILITY DRAWER, B STORMVILLE N.Y. 12 582

2. Petitioner had sexual intercourse with the above-named Respondent (on several occasions covering a period of time beginning on or about the 2 day of FEBRUARY , 1980 , and ending on or about the 7 day of JUNE , 1983 , and as a result thereof (Petitioner) (Respondent) became pregnant.

3. *(a) (Petitioner) (Respondent) gave birth to a (male) (female) child out of wedlock, on the day of 13th OF FEBRUARY, 1982 , at LINCOLN HOSPITAL BRONX NEW YORK
   *(b) (Petitioner) (Respondent) is now pregnant with a child who is likely to be born out of wedlock.

4. (Petitioner) (Respondent) who resides at G.C.FACILITY DRAWER B STORMVILLE , NEW YORK 12.582 is the father of the child.

** 5. (Petitioner) (Respondent) (has acknowledged) (acknowledges) paternity of the child (in writing) (and) (by furnishing support).

6. No previous application has been made to any Court or Judge for the relief sought herein (except

                                                                                                      .)

WHEREFORE, Petitioner prays that this Court issue a summons or warrant requiring the Respondent to show cause why the Court should not enter a declaration of paternity, an order of support*** and such other and further relief as may be appropriate under the circumstances.

Dated: JANUARY, 7th .19 93.   _Mr. Grayling Ferrand_
                                                                              Petitioner

* Alternate allegations.
** Omit if petition is filed prior to birth of child or within twenty-one years thereafter.
*** Pursuant to Section 111-g of the Social Services Law, where an order of support directs that support payments be made to the Support Collection Unit of a social services district, the petition in such proceedings shall be deemed to be an application for support services hereunder.

VERIFICATION

STATE OF NEW YORK   } ss.:
COUNTY OF _Dutchess_   }

being duly sworn, says that (s)he is the Petitioner in the above-entitled proceeding and that the foregoing petition is true to (his) (her) own knowledge, except as to matters therein stated to be alleged on information and belief and as to those matters (s)he believes it to be true.

                                                           Mr. Grayling Ferrand
                                                                              Petitioner
                                                            A.K.A. _Eugene Ferrand_

Sworn to before me this

12th day of January .1993

Richard astrother
(Deputy) Clerk of the Court
RICHARD McBYROTHER
Notary Public, State of New York
No. 01574999753
Qualified in Dutchess County 1994
Commission Expires July 27, _____

figure 1

I attended Marist College and my credits were slowly trickling in. During this time Bertha was being the faithful, loyal, and loving wife that I believed she was. Sometimes she seemed to drift off and that scared me because I had had relationships that dissolved that way. I would go get her as she drifted off and bring her back, so to speak. I would tell her to stay focused, stay strong, to have faith, and to hang in there. At other times she'd have to do the same for me.

The two youngest children, Natasha and Clinton, grew up with me behind those bars and walls. They were shy at first, but they developed a bond with me as their father that I hoped would never break. We even had a chance to spend time on the trailer visits together. They wrote me letters, and I received their report cards that we discussed sometimes. While on the visits we talked about God, life, school, responsibility and they asked me, "Daddy, when you coming home?" "Soon," I told them, "soon."

My wife was the sweetest woman I'd ever had, although she could be stubborn sometimes. We all have our shortcomings. She was a strong and dedicated black woman to have even endured that long under those circumstances and I commend her and all other women who have tried to and who are trying to do their best against all odds. We were together for three years. It would be inappropriate to mention all the good qualities that I found in my wife and none of the bad. It would also be inappropriate to air my dirty laundry in public, so to speak. I will just say that she knew what things I found distressing. I believed that things would work themselves out. There were obviously some problems, most of which were insecurities on both parts. My wife appeared reluctant to really open up and share those parts of herself that might have helped to cement our relationship a little more. I guess my reason for believing that she was holding back was based on some of my own insecurities. I demand a lot when I give a lot, which is not something that someone can readily do in some relationships. To demand a certain quantity of love or trust sounds crazy; I believe I actually try to measure that which is

immeasurable.   At that time, I was confident however that we were
going to be successful in the relationship, as long as we both kept to our
vows.

family Reunion

In August of 1993 my mother decided that she was going to come and see her son. It had been 10 years since I last saw my mother. She was also bringing my little brother Cero, who I had not seen in 10 years. First, they traveled to South Carolina to pick up my brother Adam and his twin sons. I had not seen Adam in 10 years and I had never seen my nephews, who were about 3 years old. From South Carolina they traveled to Washington, D.C. to pick up my brother Nike, who I'd seen once while on my short parole. They also picked up Nike's two children and his stepson, who is actually our nephew.

On Wednesday before I was to go on a trailer visit, they all came and visited me. There was a big table in front of us, so I could even hug them. My mother immediately had tears rolling down both of her cheeks. My system had become so immune to tears from others; I only cried sparingly, mostly for myself and for my situation because nobody seemed to cry for me, or care about me and what had happened to me. As far as I was concerned they could kill me in there and what the f--k would the President care? But it was obvious that mama still cared, even though at times I might have thought that she didn't.

My brother Nike seemed to be ready to cry as the visit ended and they were all leaving. That was a family reunion for me, and I was touched by it. It's something that I have remembered, something that could not be reversed when I finally was given my freedom. I wonder: if Charles had told the truth, would I have truly been given any type of justice? That year the family had its first reunion and I was the only member not there.

I still continued to fight and plead with the system that deliberately put me in prison to let me out. I found the appellate division and the court of appeals to be jokes because out of all the law presented to them, they had not rendered me justice. I was still there, innocent. It is a grave injustice when a society convicts someone for a crime he did not commit. It is even worse when a society goes out of its way to convict a man who they know is innocent of a crime that they know never happened. I am confident, from being there in the courtroom through that whole ordeal, that the district attorney the judge, my attorney, and possibly some of the jurors knew me to be innocent.

While serving time from 1989 to 1994 I attempted to improve myself by extracting the potential that lie inside of me. I complied with the policies and procedures of facility after facility while trying to hold on to my own ethical principles.

My brother Nike was extremely helpful to me and supportive during this time. I had met a woman that I had grown to love and respect, and whom I believed truly loved me too. There is always a margin of error when mortals attempt to judge the affairs of the heart. We were married and spent beautiful moments together, even in the mist of all that hell. Her biggest wish (and mine also) was that I come home. All and all I must say that my family, my wife, my experiences in and out of prison, and the way that I have come to perceive these series of extraordinary events have all helped in the shaping and making of the man that I am today.

Over the years, on many days and nights, while others played basketball or "kicked the willy bobo" (i.e., talked), I sat inside that prison. I thought of ways to change myself. I thought of the conditions around me and thought of changing them.

As for my daughter, she didn't really know me or recognize me as her father. I had seen her only three times in 11 years (and those times were brief). I had hoped that she and I could be like we were before, before all of the madness took place, when it was just her and me. I loved children, and I think because of my family background I was very much saddened by the fact that my daughter and I weren't closer. The fact that she didn't know me really or recognize me as her father was especially troubling for me. I had hoped for better with her. My daughter was with her maternal grandmother; Victoria's rights had been terminated long since. The agency usually received letters that I sent Too Tough and made copies of them. Too Tough didn't write back, and she had a weird perception of who I was. She wasn't told the truth about why I was in jail. I finally told her, "I was lied on. I went to trial, and I am innocent." I tried to explain as best I could to her. She expressed to me that her grandmother told her some rather bad things about me. I remember Too Tough telling me that her grandmother told her that I threw her baby milk down the toilet when she was young.

So, from then on, I concentrated mostly on my stepchildren because I guessed it would just take some time for Too Tough to come around. When and if she did, I was going to be there for her with open arms. I loved my stepchildren so much that I actually wanted to have an order of affiliation filed so that they could legally have my last name and eventually I could adopt them. The fact that their mother refused to do this lets me know that the reality was that if she left, the children would leave too. In addition, if something were to happen I could end up having to fight her other relatives for custody, or something like that. I told my stepchildren that they had a stepsister (they knew only her name). I hoped to have all of my children carry my name and live together.

Parole Board

In 1996 I went before the parole board. I had done my best to do all that I thought they would expect from me: I went to school and completed the assigned programs, and I did my best to keep my nose clean. As I waited for them to call me in, I sat with several others awaiting their fate. I was nervous. They called my alias name, "Serrando!" I got up and went inside. While sitting there, I wondered what they thought about me. Most prisoners say that the parole board has already made their decision before they meet with the convict. Finally, they spoke. They weren't mean to me at all. In fact, they were very nice. They acknowledged that I had done well in comparison to many of the other prisoners, and they spoke of my certificates. Then they asked me what happened, and as I begin to explain it was as if the whole seven years of serving time innocently caved in on me. Tears begin to flow from my eyes, like the Niagara Falls. "A crack head accused me of robbing him for $2," I told them. I told the parole board that the judge had recommended the minimum sentence for me, and he recently confirmed his previous decision that I serve no more than the minimum sentence. The board explained to me that they had to go by what was in the record and that they could not simply take my word for it. I asked myself, *then why ask me what happened if in fact it doesn't matter what I say?* The parole board listened to what I had to say, watched me cry like a baby, and then said, "You'll be hearing from us."

The Decision

The decision came in less than 48 hours: I was hit by the parole board with two more years (*figure 2*). I was extremely hurt, and my wife was devastated. I couldn't believe that the parole board could be so cruel. I thought I had done everything that was expected of me. I thought that the judge's recommendation meant something (*figure 3*).

It was no use. I had to prepare myself to serve 24 months, at least, before reappearing before the parole board. How was I going to break the news to my family, who were anticipating a positive decision? I called home to my mother and told her what happened. My mother suggested that I do some introspection and retrospection; she suggested that I look inside myself, and that I look back over my life and begin to think seriously about what I was going to do with it. I called Bertha and told her what happened. Everyone was sad and there was nothing I could do to console anyone. There was very little said between my wife and me. What could I say? What could she say?

As a result of the parole board's decision, the relationship between my wife and I began to have some serious strains on it. All of a sudden, the number of visits with her began to diminish. After a while, it appeared as though they had stopped completely. When I called home to Bertha to inquire about what was wrong, her attitude appeared to have changed. It got to the point that I could not call collect anymore and the threat of leaving became easier for Bertha to threaten me with. There were times when I felt completely helpless and I did not know what to do. It is a painful thing for an African-American man who was innocently incarcerated to feel more helpless by the nonsupport of his wife and family.

One day I received a letter from Bertha, who had not written in a while. The letter stated that she had slipped (committed adultery) and that was why she hadn't visited or written for some time. She explained that her friends suggested that she not tell me, but she felt that she had to and that she could understand it if I did not speak with her anymore, or if I did not want to be involved with her anymore.

That night I began to have nightmares and visions of another man sexing my wife. When I saw the movie *Best Man*, I had flashbacks. I told her that it was not okay, but I forgave her and needed to see her. I cannot begin to explain the psychodynamics involved in that decision. Imagine, you are incarcerated for seven years for a crime you did not commit, you are dehumanized, deprived, and there is nothing you can do about it. You have no family to come and visit you and now the one person that you think you had, you find that you are about to lose her and that another man is loving her and sexing her in ways you try not to imagine. I can only keep it real for you and say that it is a hell of a feeling to have to endure under such harsh conditions, yet it will either break you or make you. It will teach you tolerance, patience, and a defense mechanism that help you to survive another day in the battle.

It was quite a bit of time before I heard from Bertha or received a visit from her. I continued to send her the typical letters prisoners write after they have been informed that another man is sleeping with their wives:

> Honey, it is okay. I understand that you have your needs
> because you are a woman. I just want you to come up so
> that we can talk about this. I miss you. I love you, I
> love you, I love you, I love you, I love you, I love you...

After a while Bertha came back around, and I received visits and letters periodically again. I continued to work on my case and appealed the parole board's decision. I was still trying to find the complainant's witness in hopes that he might tell the truth and retract his statements.

D E C I S I O N

Denied 24 months, 5/98 Board.

Reasons: After personal interview and complete review of your
record, parole is denied based upon your continuing pattern of serious
violent crime. Your present offense (two counts of Robbery 1st
Degree) involved the in concert robbery of money from a male victim.
You punched and kicked two victims whereby he suffered a head injury
requiring six stitches. You were on parole at the time for
approximately seven months. Your criminal record commenced with a
1979 arrest that resulted in a 1983 conviction for Attempted Robbery
in the 2nd Degree. Your record totals seven violent felony
convictions and three misdemeanors. These factors belie discretionary
release. You present a serious danger to the community welfare and
safety.

The decision is above the guidelines: Due to sentence structure.
Continuous involvement with the Criminal Justice System. History of
assaultive behavior. Negative response to past correctional
influences.

Commissioner concurs.

BAK

figure 2

Supreme Court
State of New York

Jeffrey M. Atlas
Justice

Chambers
100 Centre Street
New York, N.Y. 10013

April 17, 1995

Temporary Release Committee
Fishkill Correctional Institution
Box 307
Beacon, NY 12508

Re: Eugene Serrando,
Din# 90-A-1147
Ind. 8562/89

Dear Committee Members:

I have received a letter from Neil Checkman, counsel for Eugene Serrando in which he points out to me that I recommended at Mr. Serrando's sentence that he serve no more than the minimum sentence that I imposed. Mr. Checkman also points out that the sentencing minutes state that "he should do more than the minimum".

These minutes are clearly in error. My recommendation was then and is now that Mr. Serrando serve no more than the minimum sentence.

I hope this will be helpful to you in deciding the matter.

Very truly yours,

Jeffrey M. Atlas

figure 3

Introspection, Retrospection, and Reconnection

During the time that I was writing and waiting for a response from Bertha, I contemplated the series of events that had taken place, and I did what my mother suggested I do: I began to look into myself and to look back over my life and some of things that I had done. In addition, I stayed in prayer and I began to get closer to my God. The prison that was designed to punish me, all of a sudden became a university that educated me, a womb that shaped, nurtured and birthed me back into society. Prison was the place where I became reacquainted with the God of the Universe.

My perspective began to change. I no longer wanted to do just enough to get by while incarcerated. When I went to the Alcohol and Substance Abuse Treatment (A.S.A.T.) Program, I was no longer in denial, and I took recovery seriously for the first time. As a result, I completed the program and later became a facilitator. When I went to the Alternative to Violence Program I completed the basics, the advanced, and facilitator training, and later became a facilitator for that program too. I participated in the Aggressive Replacement Training Program and later became a facilitator. I took the Network Program that focused on getting staff and participants of the program to establish a positive, growth-filled environment within prisons.

I also participated in the Inmate Liaison Committee where I became a unit representative. As a unit representative, I voiced any concerns that the unit members had to the building representative. The next election I ran for building representative, and I won. As a building representative, I gained access to the entire building in order to speak with guys in other units. During my terms as a unit representative and a building representative, I learned a little about organizational behavior and the politics associated with getting elected into office. The next term I was nominated to serve as secretary, and I won. I worked closely with the co-chairman and chairman. The next election I became the co-chairman, and eventually the chairman of the committee. As the chairman, I represented approximately 2,000 prisoners and advocated for their issues concerning medicine, food, recreation, the law library, visitations, commissary, laundry, and other issues. I also was responsible for helping to interpret policies and procedures directed to the prison population by the administration.

I took the Prisoners for AIDS Counseling and Education (PACE) Program, and received a certificate for the HIV general overview. I then went on to the next level and took the facilitator training program. I became a facilitator and later the co-chairman of the PACE program. As the co-chairman, I was instrumental in designing and implementing a 2000-hour New York State Department of Labor Apprenticeship Program (which was a collaboration of the New York State Department of Health and the New York State Department of Corrections).

I also completed many other behavior modification programs, and then I took the advance groups and facilitator training for each of those programs. I was determined to return to the parole board with more than what I had before so that they could see that I was not just doing these things for them but rather for myself.

For physical development I had a rigorous schedule where I did approximately 2,000 jumping jacks, ran approximately seven miles, did push ups, sit ups, pull ups, hit the speed bag and heavy bag, used the medicine ball, did other calisthenics, and boxed. I would hit the heavy bag so much and so hard that people always asked was I angry with somebody. In retrospect, I realize that this probably acted as stress reduction for me and as a way to suppress the pain I was feeling concerning the legal and domestic matters in my life.

I stayed busy! I completed my GED, all of the above-mentioned programs, and a four-year college degree with Marist University (majoring in psychology) while I was incarcerated. During all of this time I fellowshipped with both the Islamic and Christian faiths. I received a lot of peer pressure from both the Muslim community and the Christian community who felt that I must be crazy to religiously attend both the Christian and Islamic services. As a result of the peer pressure, I prayed harder when I went to my cell at night. By fasting with the Muslims I was in the right state to pray to God, for I sincerely wanted to worship God in Spirit and in Truth. I sincerely wanted to fast, not for flesh or to be seen of men, but rather I wanted to get closer to Jesus Christ. I wanted a personal relationship as opposed to a religion.

I cried out to the Lord day and night and asked him to increase me in knowledge, wisdom, understanding, and faith. When I think of where God has brought me from, I must confess that God is an awesome God and He has certainly increased me in every area that I asked of him. In fact, I realize today that God has always been there for me, but especially in my darkest hours. Thank you Jesus, Glory to your Holy and Precious Name. I pray that I will always respect God's Magnificent Power.

By keeping so busy, the time seemed to go by quickly and before long I was ready to go before the parole board again. By this time I had received information from the courts that confirmed that some of the information the parole board had used to hit me with more time was, in fact, erroneous (*figure 4*). The correct information was presented before the parole board. Whether or not this information persuaded the board's decision is unclear, but the decision came out favorable this time. I was granted parole.

I was so happy; it is hard to explain the feeling in words. I told the family and a few homeboys. Wise prisoners do not tell everyone in prison that they have recently been granted parole because somehow or

other negative things mysteriously seem to find their way to you, as if
something is trying to keep you there.

It is customary for inmates to leave most of their knickknacks
with their homeboys. The same night I found out I was going home I
distributed all of the things I owned to guys who were not ready to go
home. Guys received my towels, food, desktop lamp, small fan, radio,
bathrobe, and other things.

EXHIBIT 3

1.0 Broadway, Suite 500
New York, NY 10038
212.264.9940

LAW OFFICES OF NEIL B. CHECKMAN

OF COUNSEL
Eugenie H. Moody

November 15, 1994

Temporary Release Committee
Fishkill Correctional Institution
Box 307
Beacon, NY 12508

           Re: Mr. Eugene Serrando,
              DIN# 90-A-1147
              Ind. 8562/89

Dear sirs or mesdames:

      I am an attorney assigned by the Hon. Jeffrey Atlas, Justice
of the Supreme Court, New York County, to represent the above-
referenced inmate in regards to his present situation.

      Mr. Serrando is concerned that certain erroneous information
contained in his Probation Report is adversely affecting his
application for work release and parole.

      Based upon my reading of the sentencing minutes, it appears
that the complainant in the above-referenced indictment provided
false information to the Probation Department which was
incorporated in the presentence report. The complainant claimed
to have received treatment at Metropolitan Hospital for an injury
requiring six stitches.

      Upon review of the complainant's trial testimony however, it
appears that the complainant, a Mr. Carroll A. Wilder, never
received any medical treatment for this alleged injury. (See the
enclosed pages from the Trial Transcript, pp. 108-109.)

      The incident occurred on July 28, 1989. In reviewing Mr.
Wilder's Grand Jury testimony there is absolutely no mention of
the complainant receiving any stitches. In fact, there is no
mention of Mr. Wilder receiving any medical treatment whatsoever.

      Finally, I have reviewed the minutes of the sentence hearing
conducted before Justice Atlas. During that hearing, Mr. Jay
Locker, the defendant's trial attorney (now deceased), argued
that the complainant lied to the probation department about the
injuries contained in the report. The Assistant District Attorney
who was present did not contradict Mr. Locker. Of greater

figure 4: page 1

significance, Justice Atlas, who presided over the trial did not contradict Mr. Locker's assertion that the complainant lied about his injuries. This silence by those who would normally be expected to speak out, speaks volumes.

It appears that the credible evidence demonstrates that the complainant received no stitches or medical attention in connection with this incident.

In regard to Mr. Serrando's application for work release, temporary release or early parole, it appears that it was the recommendation of Judge Atlas that Mr. Serrando be granted the earliest possible release. At sentence, Justice Atlas stated: "I'm not saying the defendant should get more than what I'm going to give him. In fact, I'm going to recommend to the extent that there is a sentence, he should do [no] more than the minimum." (Sentencing minutes, p. 20, lines 18-22)[The word 'no' was omitted as a typographical error in the transcript.]

In addition, I would ask that the enclosed letters and certificates relating to how Mr. Serrando has been serving his time be reviewed by you. It would appear that he has endeavored to put his time to constructive use. This bodes well for his reintegration into society.

Should you require further information, please contact the undersigned immediately.

Thank you for your consideration of the arguments contained in this letter.

Very truly yours,

Neil B. Checkman

/NBC
encs.
cc: Hon. Jeffrey Atlas
    Mr. Eugene Serrando

figure 4 – page 2

A New Beginning

In 1998, after serving a total of nine years innocently, I was released. What was different this time from last time? I was more educated, which is important for any black man in this society, especially if he's an ex-offender. I had learned about HIV/AIDS, become a facilitator and helped to design a 2000-hour HIV/AIDS apprenticeship program with the Department of Corrections, the Department of Health, and the Department of Labor. I had participated in the Alcohol and Substance Abuse Program and then became a facilitator for the program and worked providing peer counseling to other inmates. I had taught English as a second language and learned to read, write and speak conversational Spanish. I prayed day and night and did not give up on God; I still kept the faith in my own way, in my own heart. Only God knew my true feelings. I participated in the Alternative to Violence Program and later became a facilitator. I had completed the Aggressive Replacement Training (ART) Program and later became a peer educator. The ART program focused on psychological skills training or role-playing. I had participated in and completed the Network program. I had participated in almost all the programs that were offered at the time, and I was determined to make all of that stuff pay off now that I was released.

I had developed transferable skills; I had received more knowledge, wisdom, understanding, and faith in my determination to make it in a society that said the odds were against me. In addition, I had in my mind to keep my defenses up this time. Little did I know it but I believe that God had his hands on me and his angels had already been dispatched and assigned to protect and guide me toward an appointed destination. The new beginning that I was about to embark upon was bigger than anything I could ever imagine. It was truly a plan that had already been in the making and it was not my plan but God had a purpose for my life that would come to pass.

I always use the analogy of a boxer who has boxed for 14 rounds and the trainer tells him while going into the last and final round that he is winning on every round and all the fighter needs to do is stick and move. The trainer tells the fighter to tie the opponent up if he gets to close. Stay on the bike and dance like a butterfly. The fighter goes into the fifteenth round dancing with his hands down, disregarding everything the trainer told him and gets knocked out. It is the author's belief that this is one of the reasons why the recidivism rate is so high: many people come out and be good, but they eventually let their defenses down. Once ex-offenders let their defenses down they become vulnerable to many traps and pitfalls.

The Breakup

Upon my release, I went to stay with Bertha. I was so happy to be home. There was so much I wanted to do. Bertha introduced me to a lot of her friends and family, and we had some heart-to-heart talks. However, in the back of my mind there was this ghost. I had never been delivered from the anger and hurt I felt due to the adulterous relationship Bertha had while I was incarcerated. This was one of the things that came out in our conversations. One of the things that I wanted to know was why if it was a slip did she sleep with the man more than one time? Was the second trip passion? This whole thing bothered my ego, and I could not seem to handle the betrayal.

Pressure seemed to be mounting from everywhere. These pressures included the fact that Bertha had four children and they began to say things like, "you ain't my father," and they had problems with some of the rules and regulations that I was laying down in the home. Bertha appeared to fight with me and agree with them, which did not help my feeling like an outsider. It is not an easy task for someone who had never been a father to all of a sudden become a father of four children and a grandfather.

Too Tough was in the foster care system at the time of my release. I went to see her and helped her to get out. In my mind and heart, I just wanted to be a good father to her. However, Too Tough had a problem with my separation from the Bertha because she had grown very fond of her and the children. She called them her brothers and sisters, and she was a sister to them. She called Bertha "Mommy". There came a time when Too Tough listened to Bertha over me and this caused a major problem in an already distant father and daughter relationship.

I began to feel that I had no control as the man of the house; that the woman was, in fact, attempting to establish or maintain some sense of dominance. It was not going to be easy for her to release the reins and allow me to become firmly established. I realize today that African-American women have been forced to assume command of the home and children alone for many years. They have become independent and subconsciously territorial against their own men. For some, becoming head of the household was not by choice. They had to do what they had to do, and they learned to be assertive. Unfortunately, there is a thin line between aggressiveness and assertiveness, just like there is between love and hate. No man wants his wife to hate him or be aggressive with him. Another thing that had not been considered is that we had never truly lived together because we met while I was in prison and a relationship is totally different when you have to live with a person.

Despite the trials and tribulations, I was free and determined to do what I needed to do. I had been mandated to a substance abuse program as a condition of parole, so I attended a program called New Directions. The counseling sessions seemed to only consist of the counselor asking me for ways in which I provided counseling. In other words, it appears as though he was just trying to pick my brains for knowledge about dealing with an ex-offender with substance abuse problems.

My first job was working for the Young Men's Christian Association as a site coordinator for school-aged children in the Bronx. I also decided to attend Audrey Cohen College to obtain a Masters of Science in Human Services Administration.

More problems were caused by my working and going to school; Bertha did not want me to go to school and attend the Masters program. Perhaps she wanted me to stay home more, or she just expected me to work two jobs and come home and give her all of the money, and that was it. Although I must admit that things weren't all that bad and they could have been much worse, there were a lot of issues that seemed to mount more and more. In less than one year I had purchased a brand new bedroom set for the home, purchased a computer, got Internet access, got color TV from my aunt, purchased new carpet for the bedroom, and attempted to be a good father to the children as I pretty much bought them anything they asked for. In fact I was the kind of guy that simply handed my whole check over to his wife to handle it as she saw fit. However, one day during an argument she stated that I had not done anything there. I begged to differ with her, and I reminded her of all of the aforementioned. That night, she threatened to throw me out into the street in the wee hours of the morning, and this scared me because I did not want to go back to prison. You may want to call me a momma's boy, but I called my mother and sought her consultation in this matter. My mother spoke with Bertha, and I was spared that night.

While I attended school and worked at the YMCA, I decided to seek another job. I was hired to work at Caldor's Department Store as a customer service representative. Again, I gave Bertha the check.

After about two months of working with YMCA, I was told that my fingerprints came back and due to my criminal history of attempted homicide that I had to be terminated. I explained to the employer that the attempted homicide was a cop out to get less time and that no one had been injured in the case, and, in fact, I did not attempt to kill anyone. It did not matter. I was still terminated.

To my surprise, when I lost the YMCA position, I was called for a job interview that same day with an agency called Reality House, Inc. I went for the interview and was allowed to begin as an intern student for the Masters program. Shortly after that, I was hired as a part-time counselor, and shortly after that I was hired full time. Again I give Bertha two checks (from Caldor's and Reality House, Inc.).

One day at work I received a call from Bertha saying that she needed to speak with me about something. She came to the job and said to me: "We are three months behind in rent." I was amazed because I gave her all of my money, every paycheck, plus she worked. What happened?

Bertha loved to gamble. When she finished what she had in her hand she would go to the ATM to withdraw more money to gamble with. I found this out one day when we went to Atlantic City and played a few slots. Prior to playing the slot machines, we had an understanding that the only money we had available was that which was on our person. However, Bertha went to the ATM machine at least twice when things got rough at the machines. I questioned her about this because I did not understand and I felt betrayed again. I felt that Bertha was a good woman and that I owed her so much, but I also believed that she owed me some things too because I was doing the right thing here. I was not cheating or lying, so why was I being deceived? I never received a reasonable answer for why we were three months behind in rent when I gave her money for the rent and she also worked full time. The deception became suppressed and eventually we had another heated discussion. Bertha threatened to throw me out again, and I was devastated again. I did not know what to do.

Brother 357

I decided to contact a classmate of mine who had taken a liking to me. His name was Mr. Peter Henderson, and when I told him that I was in a distressed situation he didn't hesitate to assist me. In less then 30 minutes he was tooting his horn and, to Bertha's surprise, I gave her what she asked for. The separation was instant. In less then 15 minutes my little things were packed. I only took my clothes, my books, and the computer (because I needed it for school).

Peter was married, and he had a house and an apartment. He lived alone in the apartment, so he allowed me to have the living room and a key to his apartment. He extended impeccable hospitality to me. He provided me with food, clothing, and shelter. And although he requested a minimal amount of financial assistance, I had been raised well when it came to showing appreciation for such hospitality. While living with Peter, I continued to go to school and work at Caldor's and Reality House. Caldor's went out of business, but I maintained a full-time job with Reality House.

My internship there consisted of developing constructive action to help increase the agency's census. The constructive action consisted of re-engaging outreach initiatives, and establishing new linkage agreements with agencies that were affiliated with the criminal justice system. In early 1998, the agency maintained approximately 80 clients. At this time, the agency had approximately 400 people and it continues to establish linkage agreements and other outreach initiatives to increase its census. I also worked as a HIV pre- and post-test counselor. I designed an HIV/AIDS 101 curriculum, and a Peer Educator Training Program for which the agency presently receives million-dollar funding from the Center for Disease Control, and a stipend for peer educators that have been trained. In addition, I suggested to the agency that some of the people would have unique needs based on the programmed conditioning from having been incarcerated. As a result, the agency allowed me to create a Transitional Services Program that focused on reducing recidivism by using an innovative and comprehensive approach toward treatment.

One day while traveling home on the train, two women were speaking about the New York State criminal justice system and how it was becoming more and more like an industrialized complex to warehouse African-Americans. I was just sitting there listening to them when one of them said that some brothers are incarcerated innocently. This touched a nerve, which indicates that the fear of being incarcerated innocently had cut deep. I began to explain to these women that I knew exactly what they were talking about because I had been incarcerated for something that I had not done. They told me about a place in Harlem where Leonard Jefferies was going to speak, and one of the women (Ms. Weeks) gave me her number so that we could keep in contact. I gave her a call periodically.

I completed my Masters of Science in Human Services Administration one year after being released from prison. I called Ms. Weeks to tell her that I had completed the program and had a thesis I wanted to show her. A meeting was set up for the following week. When Ms. Weeks read my thesis she told me of a homeless shelter agency that was looking for a director and a deputy director, and I should send in my resume because she believed I would be good for the position. I submitted my resume, was called for an interview and, to my surprise, I was hired as deputy director of the Eddie Harris Residential Facility.

Reality House gave me a party with ice cream and cake due to my promotion (the homeless shelter agency was doubling my salary). A few months later, I returned to Reality House to do consultant work in the evenings, three nights a week.

Can You Tell Me How I Can Get to Your House?

After the completion of the Masters program I had to wait for the degree to be signed and sent to the school. One day I went to the school to check on the status of the degree. I had been feeling kind of bad and empty because I really wanted to be settled down. I had attempted to meet young ladies but they seemed to think, "Hello, how are you doing today?" was a weak or played-out line. In any event, Peter had showed me a tactical line that might help me meet someone. On this day, I decided to try this tactic to see if it worked.

As I was walking, a couple of girls came toward me. I pulled out a fake business card and acted as if I were lost. When the young ladies drew closer, I said to one of them: "Excuse me, miss. Could you tell me," I then looked into her eyes, "how I can get to your house?" I do not know what she saw, but I got more than I bargained for. It is said that the eyes are the windows to the soul. The sight of her pretty eyes and beauty had me hooked, and a spell seemed to come over me. She smiled. I asked her name and she said in a sweet and innocent voice, "Talisa". "My name is Grayling," I told her, "and I want to speak with you later." I told her that I would come see her later. I didn't get a chance to see her right away because I had a family reunion to go to. I had never been to a family reunion and there were family members that I had not seen in over fifteen years. I was excited. So, I took off for Florida, but I still had this young lady on my mind.

Upon my return from Florida, I called Talisa and spoke with her for about 2 ½ hours, telling her my testimony. Shortly thereafter, I called and asked her if we could go out. She stated that she was going to church. "Church!" I said, "I would love to go with you." She agreed to meet with me on the outside because after my testimony she thought that

I might be a psychopathic serial killer in need of deliverance. She met with me at a gas station down the block from her home.

Things appeared to be okay during the church services until she was called up to sing a solo and the anointing of the Lord descended. The church was the Church the Temple of Blessings Church of God in Christ, a Pentecostal church located in Brooklyn, New York. I was truly moved and it was at that moment that I began to want to go to the next level in Christ.

During this time Bertha and I were communicating but I was truly afraid to go back with her after all that we had been through. Then something happened: during a casual phone conversation, Talisa told me that she was going to a wedding, so I asked her if I could come along. She stated it was all right, so we met up and went to Minister Vine's wedding. During the wedding, Sister Talisa was reminded that she had a recording to do with a gospel extravaganza, so a message needed to get to the church. When the address was mentioned, I knew that my daughter was near there. I called Too Tough and asked her to go down the block and deliver a message.

When we arrived for the recording session all hell broke loose. Somehow Bertha had been informed that I was coming to this gospel recording, and there she was with one of her friends. Bertha was there asking for Talisa and threatening to do something to her. I confronted Bertha and told her that she should not be in front of the church making a scene. She continued to be loud, boisterous, and accusatory with me. I reminded her that it was she who had thrown me out, that we were separated, that I had not done anything with this young lady, and that Talisa was a friend. Bertha continued to get so loud that I apologized to Talisa, her mother, and friends. Bertha then asked me in an arrogant voice if I wanted a divorce. I told her that I had not asked for one, but the way she was acting was pushing me. She and I continued to argue and then I told her that I wanted a divorce, and I walked away. I had committed myself, and the way I had been raised directed that you follow through once you commit yourself. What did I really know about relationships? I was away in prison during the time that most men learn about a relationship with a woman. Shortly thereafter, we divorced.

I continued to see Talisa as a friend, and I continued to attend religious services with her at the Temple of Blessings, where I became a member. It is at this time I began to get reacquainted with Jesus Christ on a more personal level. During one of the services in 1999, I asked the Lord to fill me with his Holy Spirit, and He did. Shortly thereafter, I was appointed as an amore bearer for Pastor David Grayson Jr. Approximately one year later, Pastor Grayson made me a deacon at the Temple of Blessings COGIC.

The relationship between Talisa and I continued to grow, and divorce papers were drawn up and served on Bertha. I began to tell Talisa that she had been sent to be my wife and I was meant to be her husband, she needed only to have faith. She seemed to think that I was not serious.

Things were going fine, but life is such that nothing stays the same. Things are either growing or deteriorating. While working at Eddie Harris Residential Facility, I decided to pursue a PhD in Human Services, offered online. I told the agency that I would like them to consider my candidacy for the PhD, and I would need them to allow me a few days off periodically so that I could attend residencies. I explained to the agency that I would seek to enhance the delivery of their present services and obtain additional funding. I was denied. I went to the residencies anyway and used some of my sick days. The agency then terminated me, claiming that I failed to demonstrate a willingness to cooperate with them. This did not stop me. Talisa was right in my corner.

I heard a preacher say that with every new level there is a new devil. I heard someone else say that there is no movement without friction; and someone else said that when a door closes a window will be opened.

Marriage

It was not long before I fell in love with Talisa's spirit. I felt a closeness with her that I had never felt before with any woman; it was something about her spirit. The friendship turned into dating. The divorce had gone through and people were suggesting to me not to get married again so soon. However, what is a man to do when he is in love? Before I knew it, I was telling Talisa that I loved her. She insisted that I was just going through a phase, and that I was infatuated.

The more I spoke with Talisa, the more I cared for her as a person. I welcomed the challenges of any shortcomings that she may have had and she did the same for me. One day while walking in the diamond district, I asked her to point to the engagement ring and wedding ring she thought was nice. She pointed to a set of rings that were about $5,000. I then saved up and bought the set for her. While eating dinner one day at her house, I kneeled on one knee and proposed to her, "Talisa, will you marry me?" "Yes!" she said.

We began to do just about everything together. In fact, she was made the co-chairman of RAW Ministries. She helped me to understand some things about ministry that I never knew, and she still is able to assist in her own way because she is saved, sanctified, and Holy Ghost-filled. One of the things I used to hear Talisa say is that ministry starts in the house. Talisa had been taught well; her mother is a pastor and overseer of the Jehovah Jireh Ministries Inc. Talisa and I were married on July 16, 2000.

Newlywed Trauma

A bishop once said that first there is the engagement ring, then there is the wedding ring, and after the marriage comes the boxing ring. I interpret that to mean that no marriage is perfect because we could always make our best better.

Immediately after the wedding, there were adjustments to be made; we needed to learn how to live together. We had to learn about things that dating could not prepare us for. I learned that my wife did not like sugar or other things left spilled on the counter. I learned about some of her secrets that she did not tell me during our dating, which will remain close to my chest. Several months after our wedding, my wife and I took a trip to Florida for a family reunion. During this time we went to Disney World, visited the family, and stayed in a time-share. We had a beautiful time.

When we returned home, my wife appeared to have a bit of a mood change. The mood continued, and I became concerned that she might be pregnant. Without telling her, I went to the store and bought a pregnancy test. I came home from work and handed her the pregnancy test. She looked at me like something was wrong, as if to say, "Why are you wasting your time?" I said, "Please take the test. I just have a feeling." She took the test, and it read positive. Talisa had never been pregnant before, although she had tried to conceive for many years.

Talisa could not believe it. "Something is wrong with this test," she said. "This is not correct. I have never been pregnant before. This is a cheap pregnancy test from Walgreens. You have to get the EPT original brand." "Okay," I said. "I will go right now and get one." I then purchased two EPT pregnancy tests. Talisa took the EPT again, which came back positive. She still did not want to believe the test results. She stated that she wanted to wait until the morning to test again. Nothing else was said. She was handed the other test the first thing in the morning, and it came back positive. She still did not believe it. She said she wanted to go to the doctor to be examined. She called her sister Daniele who came over to the house and said she was going to frame the pregnancy test.

Later on that day Talisa and I went to the doctor who also confirmed that she was pregnant, prescribed prenatal medication and referred her to a gynecologist. The gynecologist examined her and said all was well, with the exception of a very small fibroid.

Approximately a month later, my wife experienced bleeding, and the gynecologist was contacted. She went in to see the doctor and was told that she had miscarried due to the fibroid being in the center of her uterus. The doctor told her that he was going to remove the fibroid shortly and we could attempt to have a baby again.

About three days later, I surprised my wife with a big dinner. I had purchased some jumbo shrimp that I knew she liked and cooked them along with some yellow rice and vegetables. After eating dinner, Talisa began experiencing sharp, acute pains. She was in so much pain that she yelled and cried. I immediately called the ambulance and her gynecologist. I explained that she had just eaten dinner that included some big shrimp. While we waited for Emergency Medical Services to arrive, I spoke with the gynecologist who said that it was probably just a reaction to the D&C that was given after the miscarriage.

All along my wife continued to be in pain, and she was throwing up. After the EMS received the necessary information, they readied Talisa and took her downstairs to the ambulance. I held my newly wedded wife's hand on the way to the hospital, and for the first time I gazed into her eyes with fear in my heart. I tried to conceal this as she continued to squirm about in intense pain. It was truly a painful sight to watch.

We were about five minutes away from the Woodhull Hospital; however, we directed the EMS to take us to Brooklyn Hospital, and we arrived at the hospital approximately 35 minutes later. The minute we arrived in the emergency room, my wife screams began to intensify. In New York City the emergency rooms always appear to be filled and chaotic. I listened to my wife screaming for an additional ten minutes while information was being disseminated. I watched tears drip down her beautiful face, and I turned away to cry and wipe my tears. I then heard her yell, "Grayling! Tell him to make it stop! Honey, I am in so much pain," she said. I approached the first person with a white coat on and asked to please give my wife something for the pain. After several attempts, and my wife's constant yells, a physician came over and gave her a shot for the pain.

The doctors at the hospital were given the same information, which was that Talisa had recently miscarried and had undergone a D&C. It was explained to the doctors that she had been eating dinner and all of a sudden began experiencing sharp, acute pains in her abdomen, in her rectal area, and all up her spine. It so happened that my wife's gynecologist was an affiliate of the Brooklyn Hospital, so he was in communication with the hospital during the whole process. My wife was given many different examinations for a few days. She was examined by many doctors around the clock as they attempted to ascertain the nature of the medical problem. As the hours and days went by, it became apparent that nobody knew what was going on, and it appeared as though everyone was on a fishing expedition. One doctor came by and said that he had spoken with the gynecologist and that it was probably just an infection. A day later, we were told that the pain was just a reaction to the recent medical procedure. Shortly after that, we were told the problem was due to some food that my wife had eaten, and that our primary doctor would be in to examine her. When the primary doctor arrived and examined Talisa, food poisoning was ruled out as the cause. So, we moved from food poisoning to some reaction from the D&C to an infection and back to "Duh, I dun know." However, after several days of mass confusion and in order to save face, my wife was told that this was all due to some sort of reaction caused by the D&C procedure. She was registered to be released the next day and was prescribed strong painkillers. She was told that the fibroid would be removed in a few weeks or so, and then my wife and I could go ahead and have our baby. This would be far from the truth.

When the time came for my wife to be discharged, we refused to leave the hospital because the same pains continued to bother her. Her head was hurting, and we did not feel comfortable with leaving. Approximately three hours after the time Talisa was scheduled to be released, one of the medical staff rushed into my wife's room as if she had just discovered gold. She asked my wife how she was feeling. Talisa said that she still had a headache. The little lady stated that my wife's blood level had dropped, so it appeared as though there was some internal bleeding that no one had picked up. Things began to heat up even more. Other doctors came into the room: some looked as though they too had discovered gold, while others appeared to ask the question, "What is going on?" I heard somebody say, "The gyn is on his way." Shortly thereafter, the gynecologist arrived.

He told us that we were going to have to sign some papers and that he was going to have to operate right away. He explained that Talisa might have to have a hysterectomy and that she needed to receive at least four bags of blood immediately. The doctor still was not clear about the exact nature of what was going on. At this point, my wife and I were devastated. We had been married only a few months, and now this. We signed the papers with little choice; no time for small talk. Immediately after the receipt of the permission to operate, my wife was sped away. When I saw her again, she was on her way into the operating room. I was extremely ##########. There is no way to explain everything associated with my psychological, emotional, and spiritual being at that moment. Yet I prayed and stayed faithful in my own way.

After the operation, the doctor came out and stated that somebody must have been praying because Talisa could have died. He said that my wife had a 1-in-70000 ectopic pregnancy (i.e., one baby had begun developing in Talisa's fallopian tube while another baby had gotten stuck within one of the fallopian tubes). The one that had gotten stuck in the fallopian tube had not been detected, and as a result, it burst the fallopian tube. The doctor said that he had removed the burst fallopian tube and the fibroid at the same time. He concluded by reiterating that God was certainly watching over her. I could only think that if my wife had gone home on this doctor's orders, she would have died from internal bleeding while under the pain medication Moltrin.

Talisa was heavily sedated when she came out of the operating room. There was blood all over her abdomen where they had opened her and stitched her back up. I stayed with my wife every step of the way. When they finally put her back into her room, I refused to leave. I stayed from the beginning to the end. I slept next to her with the stitches in her stomach. Miraculously it appeared as though this helped my wife in the recovery process. In no time at all I found myself encouraging Talisa to do range of motion exercised, which she did. The next thing I knew, she was walking. Some of the nurses admired the fact that I stayed 24 hours a day with my wife. I was her emergency bell when she needed more morphine or exercise. I believe it was less than one week before my wife was released following the surgery.

No! This Can't Be Happening

When we reached home, I began to speak with Talisa about litigations against the hospital and the doctor. The doctor was a handsome young black man, and my wife thought he was very good. I agreed with her that he may have been good in some areas but he may have faltered in some other. I pleaded with her to understand that we were not medical experts, and we should allow some attorneys to review the case. I was truly concerned about the fact that my wife had almost died; and, technically speaking, we still were unaware of other potential problems. Finally, Talisa agreed to allow the litigation to begin. We received legal services from Taslim, Ruden and DiLorenz; the case in presently being litigated.

As Talisa got better, we fantasized about having our baby; we could not wait until the healing process was over. After about six months, my wife appeared to be doing great and ready for another try. One day as Talisa and I were going about our daily activities she called me and said that she was having rectal pains again. We immediately went to the hospital. We told the emergency room staff about the ectopic pregnancy and explained the nature of the pain. After hours of waiting, I asked for the patients' rights advocate in the hospital. I wrote a document that explained the nature of the pain, as well as what happened the last time this pain occurred. I had the document notarized and sent to our attorney. Shortly thereafter, a team of doctors was swarming around my wife. Tests were run, and it was discovered that Talisa, in fact, was pregnant in one of her fallopian tube. NO! This could not be happening again! It just can't be.

Again papers were signed, and my wife was sped away for another operation. The second fallopian tube was removed. What now? Due to the nature of my family background, Talisa was the only one who could carry out the Ferrand/LeGair family lineage. She felt pressured;

she was concerned that we had no biological children together. She had heard me say that I wished for a son from her.

Again, Talisa and I found ourselves enduring. We explored the possibility of doing IVF (in vitro fertilization). My wife's eggs and my sperm would be put together an attempt to get some embryos, which would then be transplanted onto my wife's womb. The question arose: where will we get the money? We did not have the medical coverage or the money to afford such a medical procedure. As a result, a loan was taken out, and we began this procedure. Talisa had to receive shots every day in her abdomen and/or buttocks. Despite the pain and aggravation that she had to go through, my wife was willing to do it for her husband. We prayed that this would work.

Finally, the day came for the eggs to be retrieved and put with the sperm in a dish. Things went well. We received a call about 24 hours later telling us that three excellent embryos had been produced. Three days later, these embryos were implanted unto my wife's womb. Now we needed to wait to see if the embryos would stick to Talisa's uterus. This would be determined after she went back for a blood pregnancy test in about 14 days.

Fourteen days later, there we were. The blood was drawn, and the anticipation was getting thicker. The doctor told us that we would receive a call later on about the results. We both waited by the phone in anticipation. Ring... Ring... Ring...

"Praise the Lord. Ferrands' residence." "Hello, this is Dr. Gracci. The results are back, and we are sorry, but the embryos did not stick. The test results are negative for pregnancy." What now? We had no more money and we still owed for the last loan taken out. The procedure would cost an additional $7,500, not including the cost of medications, which were very expensive. Though there was silence, emotional stressors spoke loudly, likened unto the power of a quiet and sincere prayer. I did not marry my wife for children, but rather I married her for her. If no children biological children are ever produced from this union, it is not her fault, and I will love her just the same.

A Granddaughter

Shortly after these incidents with the operations, our daughter Crystal (Too Tough) relapsed on drugs and left her newborn daughter at someone's house while she went off doing drugs. I received a call at my job that if I did not come and get the baby, she would be taken to the police precinct. I left work immediately. Shortly thereafter, we went to court to ensure that we had the rights necessary to get the baby the proper medical attention, etc. when necessary. We located Crystal and asked her to come to court to sign over the custody of the child until she got herself together. Likewise, the baby's father was contacted and asked his position concerning the child. The father agreed to consent to the grandparents having custody due to the fact that he could not care for the baby during his working hours, and he felt the baby would best be cared for by her grandparents. It was settled. Was this heaven-sent? Talisa quickly became attached to her grandchild. She cared for the child as if she were her very own.

The father became involved with his child's life, and he seemed very excited about it. Every weekend he provided financial support to cover the cost of the babysitter who was hired to care for the baby while Talisa and I worked.

The Fruit Doesn't Fall Too Far from the Tree

Although Crystal said that she was going to work on her treatment and do what was necessary to regain custody of her child, she did not look like she was going to succeed. She took off to Pennsylvania and rarely came to see the child. She did not send money, and she rarely called. When she did stop by, she would be dressed in very dirty clothing. Her weight began to drop. One day, we received a call that Crystal's drug addiction had become much more serious; she was using heavier drugs more often. She had hit rock bottom and wanted to come home.

It was explained to Crystal that she needed to attend a detoxification program for drugs immediately, and thereafter she would receive a treatment plan constructed by her mother and myself.

At the present time, Crystal is attempting to get herself together. She has completed the detoxification program, she attends church and is seeking help in every way that she can. My daughter still has her problems and there is room for improvement, but I am praying and believing God that she will be a powerful testimony for other young women undergoing similar struggles.

The Re-Calling:
Reaching Across the World Ministries, Inc.

As I continued to go to parole and comply with the mandates, I eventually completed the substance abuse program. Most of my parole officers appeared to encourage me to go for the PhD and to stay focused.

After a while I begin to feel a tugging at my spirit to testify of the Good News of Jesus Christ. I began to feel a need to do what I have always done for as far back as I can remember. On September 17, 2000 I realized that I had been called from the womb to be a "baptized, saved, sanctified, delivered, and filled with the Holy Ghost" servant of God.

In 2000 I was ordained as a minister, and I revisited the vision that God had given me around 1985 called Reaching Across the World Ministries. Our vision statement is "Uplifting Humanity, One Soul at a Time." This vision became incorporated in the same year and 501c(3) status was received in 2001. Our mission statement is to "Provide Faith-based Human Services Programs Geared Toward Eradicating Social Ills Effecting Humanity."

Presently, I speak in prisons, in colleges, at substance abuse programs, in homeless shelters, in public schools, and I have been on the Judge Hatchett show. I have spoken in churches when called upon to provide my testimony or to preach. I've trained staff and clients in HIV/AIDS and substance abuse related subjects. I am still pursuing my PhD in Human Services with a Specialization in Managing Non-profit Agencies at Capella University.

RAW Ministries was first conceived in approximately 1985 while I was incarcerated. I was working in the bakery at Auburn

Correctional facility. I was on a break and just thinking. That is when the complete phrase came to me because in my spirit I wanted to assist people. I wanted to help them avoid having to go through many of the things that I had gone through simply because I had grown up in a certain neighborhood or because of my ethnic background. Along with the phrase "Reaching Across the World Ministries" was the phrase I learned from the Prophet Noble Drew Ali of the Moorish Science Temple of America. They had what I'd like to think of as a vision statement: "Upliftment of Fallen Humanity." After that, I began to gather names of people for a future organization that would reach out to people around the world. I told them that I was going to have something in place to help brothers and sisters when they get out of prison. I had no idea how I was going to do it, or what that something would be.

Shortly thereafter, I began to develop an organizational flowchart. As I look back now, I believe it was God guiding me, and I was just a vessel. I had the desire in my heart to work toward helping people who were less fortunate; however, I did not know which methodology I needed to use to raise the money that would be needed to purchase property that would allow me to house the homeless in general, and the homeless ex-convict specifically. My conditioning to a stinking way of thinking was just lying dormant in my subconscious mind. Upon my first release after doing 6 to18 years, the vision and dream were still there, but plan of action was not sound. Moreover, I did not have on the armor of God (Ephesians 6). I found myself desperate, and I decided that I would organize the old crew and lock down a bunch of blocks with red tops, black tops, and anything else that would allow me to raise a lot of money. In my mind I was going to be the Robin Hood of the hood. However, there was a lesson to be learned, and that lesson was that the safest place is in the will of God. Sometimes we just have to wait on God.

I eventually fell victim to the lifestyle of selling drugs and getting high, which placed me in a circle of people, places, and things that are ripe for the first-time offender to become a repeat offender. I was falsely accused, and spirited back to prison. The dream of RAW was deferred. Less than six months later, I was back in prison in July of 1989. The vision of RAW would resurface from the attic of my mind about two years later while incarcerated. Again, I began to gather names and discuss my vision of reaching across the world. Most of the time people laughed at me and did not take it seriously. Some guys just gave me their phone number in case I was paroled before them in hopes that I would send them a package.

Upon my release in 1998, I had all of the phone numbers and the concepts of RAW that I had written in the wee hours of the morning as I listened to the sniffles of men crying in the darkness in winter, spring, summer, and fall. A bittersweet sound because, for some, this may have been when they were humbly crying for help. There were other crying sounds, but they were more like agony then anything bittersweet. You know what I mean.

So upon my release in 1998, RAW was still not at the surface but it was not gone. The seed was planted in 1985 and watered while incarcerated from 1989 to 1998. All that was needed was for God to give the increase. The next year after my release, while I was in church with my fiancée at the time, I heard the pastor preaching. He stated that he had never smoked a joint (marijuana), he had never taken a drink of alcohol, he had never been in prison or used any drugs, his grandfather was a preacher, his father is a bishop, and he was the pastor now. At this time, I felt like Paul who had been struck by a light on his way to Damascus! It was as if God's spirit was talking to me:

> "It is I who has spared your life, who has brought you
> out of the darkness into the marvelous light! It is I who
> has allowed you to see things that some pastors will
> never see! It is I who has picked you up out of the muck
> and the mire and has cleaned you up for my Glory. It is

I who gave you the vision of Reaching Across the World Ministries! It is I who now sends you forth to preach the Gospel and testify of the miracle that I have bestowed upon you. Tell how you were once blind and now you see; how it was grace that saved you from a lifestyle of destruction where from the blindness of your rage you were running upon destruction! Tell how you were humbled even during your innocence in prison; how you waited upon me; and how you blessed me even during your trials and tribulations. You are commissioned and ordained to go forth, not by man but by me. I have shaped you and molded you for a time such at this.

I felt as if there was a fire shut up in my bones. The vision of RAW Ministries just resurfaced. I began to tell everyone. I told the pastor of that church, who said he had not heard from God yet. I did not want to be disobedient, so I explained to the pastor as best I could that there were people who were suffering and they needed to know that they did not have to suffer anymore because Christ is the answer, and He had come so that they could have life and have it more abundantly. As I learned more about the ministry and the different denominations and traditions in the modern-day church, I knew that I could not function under some of the traditional ways that were set up. Another scriptural verse came to me; "He that believeth on me the works that I do shall he do also, and greater things then these shall he do, because I go unto my father". I did not understand it yet, but I was quickly learning that God always will make a way out of what appears to be no way. He is Jehovah Jireh, he will provide the same way he provided the ram for Abraham. He may not come when you want him to, but he is always right on time. I told my wife about the vision and what God had spoken to me, and I told her mother. She and her mother were very supportive. They said, "If God told you to, then go! You better get to going," and I have been running with the vision ever since.

I was ordained by my mother-in-law, Overseer Frieda Harrison of the Jehovah Jireh Ministries, Inc. RAW Ministries became incorporated on September 17, 2000. The next day, the Holy Spirit moved me to meet an evangelist named Ollie Ross. That day, she gave me the key to the prayer room that was going to be used to offer children bible lessons on Saturdays, as a starter. We began with two children (who are twins). Shortly thereafter, we had about 15 children and a choir had formed. We began singing at church functions, and a few more children were added. We then obtained our tax-exempt status from the Internal Revenue Service.

People began to hear about us in the community and we were given an honorarium from Assemblyman Vito Lopez' office in August 2002 for the work we had been doing in the community. We started to receive former prisoners who came to us to assist them with resumes, job referrals, etc. I was being asked to speak at prison facilities, schools, and chemical dependency agencies. However, RAW was still limited because we did not have our own space to operate out of. We still did not have any funding from the government or private corporations. We relied solely on the salaries that my wife and I made. We then reached out and started to receive snacks from the supermarket, a once-a-month meal from McDonalds. God began to do it again (i.e., provide) for the ministry.

Then I heard about the New York City Housing Preservation Department and made contact with someone who was working there. This led to my obtaining a listing of the sites that were available to be rented. I looked at approximately four different places before finally settling on a site at 1237 DeKalb Avenue in Brooklyn, New York. I spoke with HPD, who sent the individual disclosure form, the entity disclosure form, and some other documents that I needed to fill out. They also asked that I purchase a certificate of liability. I did not know how I was going to get this; but again, God made a way. I began to get candy wholesale to use to request donations for the purchasing of the certificate of liability (which cost $1,200). It took less than a week for me to raise the money for the certificate. I purchased it, and then had to wait for the appraisal to be completed. Although we needed microphones, chairs, the floor to be done, some wiring, sheet rocking, etc., we believed that God was going to provide for us, and we anticipated and had a successful grand opening on August 31, 2003 at 1237 DeKalb Avenue. At the same time, I received a call from the New York State Department of Parole informing me that I have been discharged from parole. This was perfect timing because this allows me to be able to travel and minister throughout the states.

It wasn't long before the Holy Spirit reminded me of this book, which has been given as a gift to make way for the ministry. RAW Ministries envisions "Humanity Uplifted, One Soul at a Time", for it is the soul that must be saved above all else. The ministry has a mission to assist mankind by helping to reduce the socio-cultural ills that affect humankind.

The future direction of Reaching Across the World Ministries, Inc. is to network, collaborate, and link with others who desire to make preparations for the next generation. We strive to develop and implement faith-based human services programs, which are geared toward eradicating those things that cause moral and social decay of the individual, families, communities, and society at large.

It is hoped that this autobiography will be picked up by a playwright or film director and turned into a play or movie. Denzel (Washington) would be great in this one. It is hoped that this book will receive favorable media coverage by local radio stations, news stations, and local and national periodicals. It is hoped that talk shows will embrace the message under the words and provide their assistance by inviting us to be on their shows: *Like It Is*, *Oprah!*, *Montel Williams*, *60 Minutes*, *Maurey Povich*, *Larry King Live*, and others. It is hoped that in the future I may be able to speak encouraging words to people in colleges, high schools, homeless shelters, chemical dependency agencies, prisons (city, state, and federal), churches, and community-based organizations nationally, and ultimately internationally.

It is hoped that grade schools, universities, and doctoral programs will embrace this autobiography and integrate it into their curricula as a text requirement.

Again, thank you all for your support and God bless you.

Epilogue

Things are still bad for the black nation (and our nation in general) despite our ability to be resilient. What we must do is pull together, somehow, to seek and find workable solutions that we can implement with the slightest of ease. Don't get me wrong, there are a lot of people out there that are and have been trying to do this. However we must begin to recognize those individuals who are right around us putting forth time and effort to help in our struggle for betterment. Let us join in with our brothers and sisters to uplift our families and all of humanity.

I believe that we have been arguing the question for centuries of whose God is the absolute truth; this has caused us to lose a lot of ground. I don't advocate termination of religion, but rather more tolerance of each others' perspectives, and like Malcolm X said, set our religions aside so that we can come together on some of the things we have in common [paraphrasing].

Unfortunately, we (black people) appear to be regressing as a people, although it couldn't be seen as such when we view some of our black talk shows, and other black programming on television. However, when we take a closer look at the many other things that plague our society as a whole, and particularly in the black family, we then begin to see how farther and farther away from our natural order we have come. According to the Department of Health, African- Americans are disproportionately infected and affected by the spread of HIV; it is the number one killer for young African-American women aged 18 through 44; the quickest population contracting HIV demographically speaking are young African-American men! And more than 90 percent of the babies born with HIV in the State of New York are African-American and Latino- American. Listen to the rap music that our children are listening to. Many of the artists who sing these songs are often featured on the front cover of magazines. The so-called notorious 50% and gangster rap may be a ticket out of the ghetto for some, but at what price? The Bible asks the question: "What does it profit a man to gain the world and lose his soul?"

I have seen a brother ask a sister who was addicted to crack to perform oral sex on a dog in the street amongst spectators. He said he did it just for fun. It's sad for a brother to get enjoyment out of doing something like that to a sister.

The books *Black Man's Guide to Understanding the Black Woman* and *Black Woman's Guide to Understanding the Black Man* imply that we need some guidance in understanding what has happened or what is going on with the black female-male relationship. Not to say that there aren't any working relationships because I am sure that there are many, but I have watched some of the videos depicting what young black men think of black women, and I have watched videos where young black women strike back at young black men. This can be seen in a lot in rap videos. This society perpetuates a certain type of mentality that many of our women and men follow. For example, if we watch the soap operas and listen to many of the radio talk shows and TV talk shows, we will pick up a certain mentality that is none other than a conditioning of our society. The black woman and the black man have lost some of the respect they had started to gain in the early sixties. They call themselves "b--ches with attitudes," "niggers with attitudes," etc. They show you in their videos that it is about using your friend or man for material gain, and basically prostituting one's body.

Sexual exploitation of both men and women is on the rise and, in fact, is normal in this society. Our women think that it is perfectly normal and okay to go to male strip shows and allow men to swing their private parts all in their faces while they sit there and lust. Black men today are being used by a lot of women as male prostitutes. You can go buy sexual favors from a man just as quickly as you can from a woman. I don't say that it is correct for either, and I am not suggesting that either sex is at fault for the direction of destruction that we are in, but rather I hope that we acknowledge the seriousness of our situation before it is too late. We must pick ourselves up out of the gutter. If we are men and we see a woman down and out, we don't have to exploit her; and the same goes for the women who would exploit the brothers. Like Dr. Frances Welsing said: we are on the same team, and it is not for the black king to slap the black queen or the black queen to slap the black king; but rather we work together against our opposition, whatever or whoever that may be. If we can straighten out our families, our generations will begin to live a more moral life. This doesn't just apply to black people, but all people who desire to rise above that which would bring them, their families, and their nation down.

I have found it hard to reconcile and forgive much less forget the trials and tribulations that my ancestors were forced to endure. However, I have found myself going through a transformation where I realize that the newer generations have had nothing to do directly with what their ancestors did to my ancestors. It is unfair to blame them and I believe that the dreams of Dr. Martin Luther King Jr., Gandhi, and many other men who advocated peace can made reality if we as the human race begins to strive toward this objective. Hence, I feel I have gone through a transformation, although some may see this as a sellout. It is not. I was in jail serving time because of a system that has its designs. I don't say that institutional racism doesn't exist. What I am learning is that many people will bare witness to the truth if the truth is brought with the proper approach, and many people want to do right despite certain "powers that be" projecting falsehood via the media. Future generations will have to decide what they will do. I say to them: Be your own man. Make your own decision and defend your own realities. Most of all, keep it real.

In keeping it real, I must look at all the possibilities before making a decision and acting. The black man who is an ex-convict has to consider that it is possible that, although he prepared for a successful re-entry into society, he may run into a brick wall despite all his planning. The question is: then what? What does an ex-convict do when he is back to square one? If we agree that this is a possibility, we should then therefore look at our options. We should develop our old skills while incarcerated, if it comes down to that. We must realize that it is about survival, and we cannot afford to be going back to prison, especially the "three strikes and you are in for life" policy.

I am not saying that one shouldn't take advantage of the obsolete training that the New York State Department of Corrections offers at some jails. For example, some of the auto shops are training prisoners to work on cars as old as 1965, where in today's society and with the advancement of technology cars are being computerized. Therefore the convict is only being made ill prepared, though he is given the illusion that he is being prepared. The same is true when the parole board tells a 55-year-old man that he should go and obtain his GED before he could be released or a 60-year-old man to earn a two-year degree. The truth is that any black man who is getting out of prison with 5, 10, 15 years of incarceration and he is going out there looking for someone to give him a job may be in for a rude awakening. He must prepare himself on all levels, including resorting back to his old trade, if need be. He must be prepared to make his own employment somehow. As ironic as it may sound, he may need to learn more about how not to make the mistake(s) he made before in the event that he has to resort back to what he knows best. Unfortunately, many brothers go home with the illusion that they are going to be hired and get a good paying job to support them and their families. We must look at the whole picture and not just half. Take, for example, the following situation: You are a plantation owner and you have slaves on your plantation who pick cotton and do other manual labor, etc. You decide you need another strong buck with potential. As a result, you go to the auction where you are given the choice of two black men. One is 21 years old and looks like a bodybuilder, and the other is 62 years old and looks every bit of 82 because of his rough life. Both are being sold for $5. Which one would you most likely buy? The black ex-convict is faced with the same situation, only on a more modern level. There are people out in society who have no criminal history with the same two-year degree that you as an ex-convict obtained. There are 20-year-old men with the same degree you have and they, too, are applying for a job; the company may see a future with the 20-year-old guy, but may see a liability with you. To add to this, we have the all-too-well-known white institutionalized racism and the stigma attached to being an ex-con.

So here we see the possibility of being left with very few options. If we buy into the illusions that we receive from the prison administration that works hand-in-hand with the white institutionalized racist system, we will have a greater chance of going back to prison and being a statistic. We must develop networks and use them to help our people. I advise people in prison to get all the education that they can. In addition, I advise them to learn things from those brothers around them, including the elder brothers whom we seem to have gotten away from somehow.

The reality is that we must keep things real. We must teach the youth in prison that if they are going to do wrong they are going to have to suffer the personal, family, community and social consequences of their actions. In other words, instead of teaching them to do wrong better, just teach them to do right. I pray that this book will act as an intervention in which many of the youth of today do not make the same mistakes I have made. Youth must understand the importance of organizing and nation building. They need to know how to manipulate in our society so they can be successful. Everyone loves a winner in this society. Our plight is such that it is inevitable that there will be divergent perspectives on how to help us get out of the muck and the mire as a nation. We must find a way to administer our resources despite our many differences. Can we work together as Muslims, Christians and Jews? Can we organize, strategize, galvanize and utilize those members of society labeled as thugs (i.e., Bloods, Nieta's, Latin Kings, Crips, etc.? Many may think that to consider such union is a work of the devil. However, the Jesus didn't come for the safe, but rather he came for the sinner. Moreover, Jesus having sat with the tax collector appears to have been a strategic move because that act ultimately ended in the tax collector becoming one of the original disciples, (i.e., Matthew). Again, we will have divergent methods and ideas on how to reach a particular end; how we receive one another and our ability to place the best construction on each other's concepts will be crucial in determining acceptance. There was a time when I would say we must use all we can to find our way back home, even if it means to improve on our method of committing criminal acts. This is because I was taught, "If you are going to be a street sweeper, be the best street sweeper you can be," and I related this to selling drugs and committing crime. However, I understand now that we must teach our children to stand up for something, or they will go for anything. We must teach them to understand the importance of having the practical application of academic and spiritual information. The question was asked, "What does it profit a man to gain the world and lose his soul?" This is God's way of cautioning us to stay within a certain boundary despite how rough things appear to be. The home I speak about is that simple life that most black people look for: having peace of mind and being able to have sufficient income for food, clothing, and shelter, with the added touches of the finer things in life. If a person allows himself to go hungry, be outdoors, and naked, that is his choice, but I cannot condemn the man who tries to uplift himself from this state of existence. We must stop looking at life from an illusionary perspective.

We constantly hear about the war on drugs and crime. Billions of dollars of the taxpayers' money are going toward the effort to fight crime and to put another 100,000 police into the community. This is the kind of money you use from a war chest; this is the amount of men you send in on a war mission. Wake up! Who are the targets? What is the mission? The truth is that these troops are going in to the black community and black people are the targets. Remove the illusion and keep it real. I never thought of becoming a millionaire, even when I was selling drugs. I just lived for the day, basically. However, I know that all things are possible with God-- for if He be for me, who can be against me? One of my dreams is to begin to implement some of the things that I envision into the concepts of RAW. I realize that it will take money to do a lot of the things that I have planned, and certainly it will take finances to uplift a nation of people to the level of things made manifested in the physical realm. I am calling on all of those who want to help, to help me. I thank you and I appreciate your giving me this chance to speak to your mind and hearts. God Bless.